WILMA ELLERSIEK

DANCING HAND – TROTTING PONY
Hand Gesture Games, Songs and Movement Games
for Children in Kindergarten and the Lower Grades

TRANSLATED AND EDITED BY
LYN AND KUNDRY WILLWERTH

WITH A CONTRIBUTION BY
INGRID WEIDENFELD

WALDORF EARLY CHILDHOOD ASSOCIATION OF NORTH AMERICA

Acknowledgments

This publication was made possible by a grant from the Waldorf Curriculum Fund.

Selection, preparation and translation of the original German texts, songs and games were made possible in part, by a grant from the International Waldorf Kindergarten Association.

The first editions of the original German texts were published under the titles, *Die Tanzende, Spielende Hand* and *Wer Schleicht heran mit Leiser Tatz* by Wilma Ellersiek, Verlag Freies Geistesleben & Urachhaus, Stuttgart. Copyright © Verlag Freies Geistesleben & Urachhaus, GmbH, Stuttgart, Germany, 2004 and 2005.

This English edition contains most of the material from the German edition, selected, edited and translated by Kundry and Lyn Willwerth.

This edited English translation copyright © Waldorf Early Childhood Association of North America, 2010.

Published by Waldorf Early Childhood Association of North America (WECAN) 285 Hungry Hollow Road, Spring Valley, New York 10977 USA.

ISBN: 978-1-936849-41-3

10 9 8 7 6 5 4 3 2 1

Illustration and cover: Friedericke Lögters
Musical notations: Ingrid Weidenfeld Design and
typeset: Roland Willwerth Printed by:
Alphagraphics, Pittsburgh, PA, USA

All rights reserved. No part of this book may be reproduced in any form without the written permission of the publisher, except for brief quotations in book reviews and articles.
Printed in the United States of America

Table of Contents

Introduction — vii
  Translator's Foreword — vii
  Additional Animal Games in
  Previous Books by Wilma Ellersiek — viii

Preface — 13
  The Experience of Rhythm
  in the First Seven Years of Childhood — 13
  Mood of the Fifth with Central Tone A — 14
  The Practice of Singing — 15

Part I: The Playing, Dancing Hand — 16
  Let's Play and Dance — 16

  Group 1: Games for Fists — 17
    Molla Moolla — 18
    Croll and Crooll — 21
    Pum and Pom — 26

  Group 2: Games for Thumbs and Fingers — 31
    Tom and Tim — 32
    Boomsti! Woomsti! — 35
    Flip and Flop I — 38
    Flip and Flop II — 41
      Round-a-Ring — 41
    Pips and Pops — 45
    Bala Bane — 49
    Nicky — 52

  Group 3: Games for Hands Alternating with Fingers — 56
    Oolla Woolla — 57
    So Play My Hands — 60
    Weedle Woodle — 64
    Trip by Boat — 67
    Tompa-Tempa I — 71
    Tompa-Tempa II — 74
    Mock and Pock — 77

Part II: Trotting Pony   **80**
  Poem: All Creatures We Love   80
  About Children and Animals   81
  Poem: Living Water and Bread of Life   83

  The Earthworm   84
  The Snail   87
  Hustle Hoosh!   89
  The Cat   93
  Flutter Flutter   96
    Loo-loo-loo   100
  The Birdie   101
    Tiree-dee-dee   102
    Blow, Blow, Wind so Mild   102
  The Birdie Movement Game   108
  Quiet-as-a-Mouse – Hoppa-Hop   109
    Wind-soo-soo   110
  The Little Fish   116
  The Doggy Tapple-Tapples   119
  The Honey Bee   124
    Sirra-hum   124
  The Little Bear   128
  So Runs My Pony   133
  The Little Donkey   138
    Tep-tep-tep, with Gentle Step   138
    It is enough!   139
  Quawkalone and Brummelbone   148
  Before Dawn—Wake up!   153

Appendices   **158**
  Jingle Stick Directions   158
  Wilma Ellersiek, a Life for Rhythm   159
  Addresses   161

Dedicated in loving memory of Lyn S. Willwerth

INTRODUCTION

Translator's Foreword

In this, the long-awaited fourth volume of hand gesture and movement games by Wilma Ellersiek, the joyful and humorous "Dancing Hand" games are now available, bringing laughter and fun to your play with children. Though full of lively movements and unforeseen incidents, they demand thoughtful concentration in their presentation in word and movement.

A second group of games is also presented here: animal games. These are magical. They transform us into the guise of snail, worm, bunny, pony, and many other creatures. For a little while we can dance as bunnies or fly as birds, seeking food and drink and giving thanks in song, going "tep-tep-tep with gentle step" as little donkeys up the mountain.

Only with practice can we actually move in the many ways of our animal friends and invite the children to join us. In the beginning, we must work diligently to combine word and movement harmoniously. But the children reward our efforts by joyfully playing along with us. And as we master one game after the next, the task of learning them becomes easier. We can feel within us the healing force of these games, a force that we can impart to the children in joyful play.

In this way Wilma Ellersiek, in her hand gesture and movement games, offers us play material that takes account of the new medical research into the connection between hand and brain. The games develop the power of imitation, a force underlying all pre-school learning. Ellersiek also opens the way to rhythmic experience in singing and in melodious speaking. She leads us to the wellspring of the joy of existence and active participation with the world around us.

Since Wilma Ellersiek began creating these musically formed and structured games thirty years ago, interest has been shown in this work for children around the globe. Not only in Europe, but all the way to Russia, and as far as India, China and Korea, as well as Australia, New Zealand, and here in the Americas, children enjoy her games. The "Dancing Hand" can do its tricks to rhythmic sound syllables and songs, beyond the conceptual word, and the sound of animals can accompany their movements in many languages. Efforts at translation are also widespread, by our Spanish and Portuguese-speaking neighbors as well as by kindergarten teachers in other countries.

We hope that this English translation will be the forerunner for many Ellersiek games in languages around the world, and encourage translators to bring them to the children in their own language.

Additional Animal Games in Previous Books by Wilma Ellersiek:

Giving Love – Bringing Joy:
  Snailyman (a)
  Crawly-Crawl (a)
  Bzzz (a)
  Visitor (a)
  Burra-fuzz (a)

Gesture Games for Spring and Summer:
  Easter-Fun (a,d)
  Hoppa Hoosh! (b,d)
  Winging, Winging (b,d)
  Bird Concert (a,d)
  The Little Woodpecker (b,d)
  The Flower in My Garden (a)
  Our Lovely Earth (a,c,d)
  Rain Song (b,d)

Gesture Games for Autumn and Winter:
  What Do Animals Do in the Snow?
  Polar Bear (c,d)
  Little Mice in the Snow (c, d)
  Birdie in the Snow (c,d)

a = hand gesture game
b = hand gesture or moving game with song
c = moving game
d = games suitable for combination with other games

PREFACE

The Experience of Rhythm in the First Seven Years of Childhood

The feeling of rhythm in the first seven years is fundamental, based on pulsation. Pulsation is the initial element, the germinal cell of all rhythmic activity. It is the constant repetition of what is similar, yet not identical. Pulsation is the basic beat, oriented to the heartbeat, dividing the stream of time.

Pulsation has two aspects: it is the polarity between stress and relief, impulse and relaxation (usually denoted as "pause" or "rest"), in which something decisive occurs, namely the preparation for another impulse. The heartbeat also has two parts: a polarity of expansion and contraction (systole and diastole); in the same way, breathing has its polarity of exhalation and inhalation. Like pulse and breathing, pulsation is variable in tempo; like these it has an elastic ability to adjust and can become slower or faster, thus working as an enlivening element in time's flow. Pulsation forms the basis for all ordering of time.

In spite of the action of its movement, there is nothing merely mechanical about pulsation. It has nothing to do with the usual time counting music teachers use to accustom their pupils to a regular tempo, often with the well-known mechanical metronome as its basis. This mechanical metrical tempo measurement is a linear, non-living rate per second in which the "beat" is hammered out, partitioning, but carrying no forward movement such as one finds in the stress of pulsation. Through the metrical time-measure, all living streaming and breathing is destroyed. It has a deadly effect on all musical execution.

The precision of pulsation is different from that of the machine. It responds not to mechanical laws, but to those of life. Therefore it is not fixed, or monotonous; it is elastic in its constant alternation between phases of stress and relief.

Graphically illustrated:
Meter: ‑ ‑ ‑ ‑ ‑ ‑ ‑ ‑ ‑ ‑ ‑ ‑ ‑ ‑ ‑ ‑ ‑
Beat: • ‑ ‑ ‑ • ‑ ‑ ‑ • ‑ ‑ ‑ • ‑ ‑ ‑ • ‑ ‑ ‑
Pulsation ∿∿∿∿∿∿∿∿∿∿∿∿∿∿

In the first seven years of life, the blood circulation and breathing only gradually become coordinated. A rhythmic relationship only slowly becomes established and stable. (This process actually only comes to its final equilibrium around the ninth year of life.) For this reason, one should spare children in this stage of life the rule of measure, beat, and fixed note value, for these are a harmful, disturbing, even destructive interference for the child.

Movement, speech and song should be brought to the child as pulsating activity in support of the building up of the bodily organism and its functions. This especially concerns the lullabies.

Mood Of The Fifth With Central Tone A

Pentatonic melodies can only move in a swinging motion around a central tone. They float, without a stressed beginning and without tending toward a resolved end. They expand in a spiral or in increasing circles and constantly swing back within their own boundaries. They play with tones and are intoning play.

Fritz Jöde

Mood of the fifth with central tone A corresponds to the cosmic experience of childen in the first seven years, who are still at one with the world and do not yet feel a polarity between it and themselves. This musical mode forms a protective shelter in which the child can feel secure.

Mood of the fifth signifies unity with the cosmos, in which heavens and earth are yet united. It means being in harmony with a divine center.

It is a tonal space of optimal balance. All tones of the upper and lower fifth intervals are equally far removed from the central tone A. The entire space comprises not an octave but a ninth-interval in which everything is in balance.

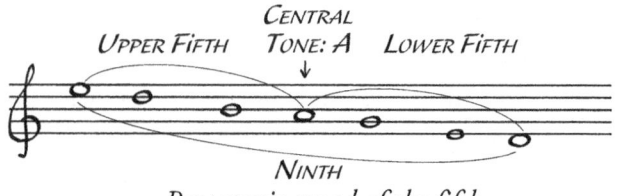

*Pentatonic mood of the fifth
(original ancient Greek form) with central tone A*

The diatonic scale has a different structure: there are two centers. Contrast is established between the fundamental tone and its octave. Half-tones, minor and major thirds give rise to minor and major modes with their respective feminine and masculine characters. From this springs the phenomenon of duality with the world, contrasting with the unity achieved through the mood of the fifth. In the songs for the first seven years of life, this duality should not yet be broached.

The entrance of the third, major and minor, makes it possible for human beings to come to know their inner lives, to comprehend themselves within their feelings. This offers the possibility of imposing limits on oneself, which represents progress in development. It is not hard to see how harm can ensue if the tendency for self-limitation is promoted in a child, for whom unity with the world is the needed basis for healthy development.

In the songs published here this need of the children is fully and entirely considered. According to manifold experience, the exclusive presentation of mood of the fifth motifs and melodies, brings about a profound recovery and healing from the harmful influences to which the child is exposed in his or her surroundings.

The Practice of Singing

It needs to be mentioned that the adult should approach the child very carefully with lullabies and melodic motifs. Singing should be *sotto voce* without vibrato. The tone glides on the breath stream, surrounding, rather than gripping the child. The rocking movement and the singing of the words must be embedded in a pulsating flow.[1] The singing is not meant to impress, but to form a shelter into which the child can nestle. To do this, all sentimentality and emphasis on the textual meaning need to be avoided. The flow of sound is to be given objectively, making possible the feeling of cosmic order.

Finding the Pitch for Singing

If one is not sure of being able to sing an A freely by ear, one may avail oneself of one of the Choroi instruments: interval flute, brass tone bar, kinderharp. Calmly play the tone A to the children, then humming or singing "la-la," let the tone continue. Singing the tone A to the children is essential; it engages them in the tonality and provides the needed basis for singing.

---

[1] See "The Experience of Rhythm," p. 13.

Part I: The Playing, Dancing Hand

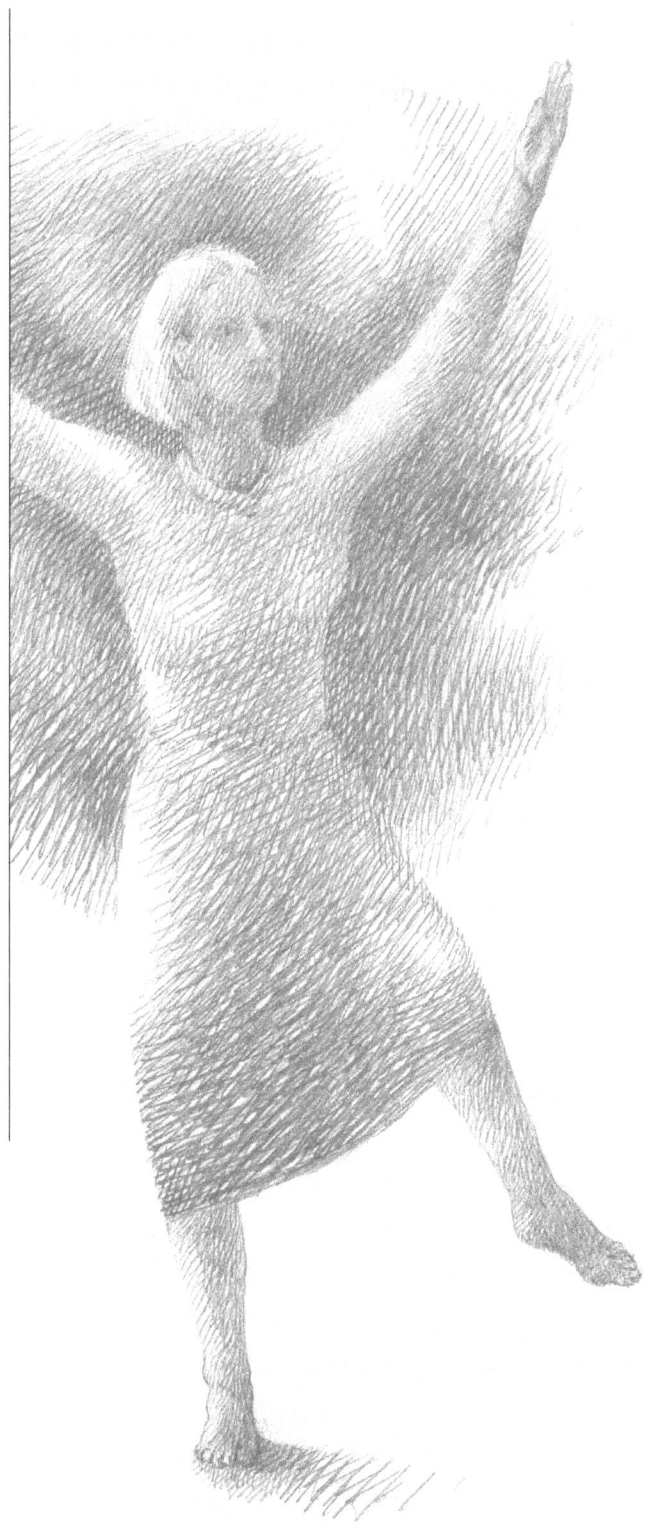

Let's Play and Dance

In our kindergarten at Hillside we often welcome visitors. Some of the ones that are the most fun to play with come in pairs. There are Pum and Pom, for instance. They show us how to jump and climb and don't mind if we laugh when they fall down into the mud. Croll and Crool help us wind the wool for our hand knitting, except they are very silly and wind an enormous ball, to which they give a push, and oops, it rolls away, never to come back. Wait, it's not quite that bad! They find the tail end nearby, and can wind the whole enormous ball back again! And there are other friends who come to visit and involve us in all sorts of escapades.

Well, you wonder, why do you allow these characters with all their foibles into the kindergarten or even your home? I'll whisper it to you: They are finger friends, thumb friends, fist friends, all ready to play. Each pair has a verse by Wilma Ellersiek that shows them how to play with us, to give expression to their actions. Whoosh – they fall down; bob – they bump each other. They roll and stretch to rhythmic speech, they whirl, wobble and pull.

Before we know it, our own fingers are doing likewise. What a contrast! First we dance around the ring, then we waddle in place from side to side, then we jump up and down, always the pair, but along with many other pairs. Take care: one of them might get stuck in a sack, or all get dumped overboard in a storm! Manifold adventures await us when Wilma Ellersiek takes us along on one of her finger journeys. And in the end our brain receives a massage, its connections vibrating with activity in concert with our finger-dance!

We thank you, Wilma Ellersiek, for all the fun we can have with our dancing hands, toys we have with us wherever we go, and for sharing your humor and joy when you sent us your finger friends.

Kundry Willwerth

GROUP I: GAMES FOR FISTS

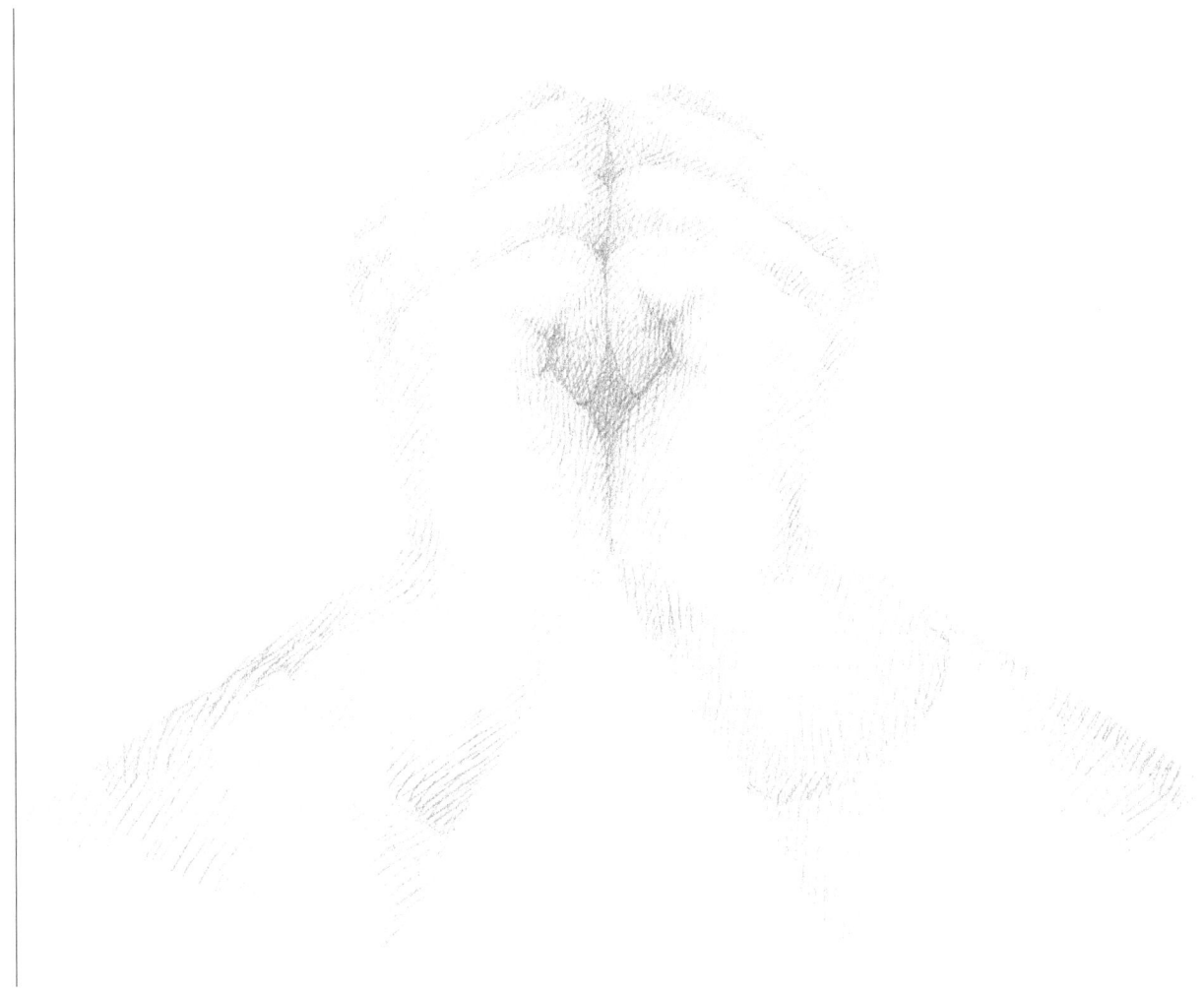

Molla Moolla
Sound-Syllable Game for Fists

Molla – moolla – molla – moolla,
Molla – moolla – molla – moolla:
  Poom – poom – pah!
  Poom – poom – pah!
Molla – moolla – molla – moolla,
Molla – moolla – molla – moolla:
  Hoppala! Hoppala!
Molla – moolla – molla – moolla,
Molla – moolla – molla – moolla:
  Pom – pom – peck!
  Pom – pom – pawn!
Molla – moolla – molla – moolla,
Molla – moolla – molla – moolla:
  Whoops! And gone!
  All gone!

TEXT:

1 Molla – moolla –
    r   /
           molla – moolla,
            r   /
Molla – moolla –
    r   /
           molla – moolla:
            r   /

MOVEMENTS:

1 Form loose fists with both of your hands; your thumbs lie on top of your fingers. Hold your hands before you at about stomach height, with the backs of your hands towards the children and your right fist above your left fist. Now turn your fists around each other in a flowing movement with the speech rhythm. The children will move their fists in a free rhythm. This is expected and must not be corrected.

PRONUNCIATION:

Moolla and poom: short oo as in book.

This game is so composed that its effect on the children is liberating and ordering, calming and awakening at the same time.

In the repetitive "molla – moolla" verses children experience a joy in movement. During the verses in "pum – pum – pah!," "hoppala," "pom – pom – peck!," a more controlled movement is introduced; then in "pom – pom – peck!," the children experience a physical calming.

2   Poom – poom – pah!
      Poom – poom – pah!

3   Molla – moolla –
       r   /
             molla – moolla,
               r   /
     Molla – moolla –
       r   /
             molla – moolla:
               r   /

4   Hoppa-la! Hoppa-la! –
      ↓ ↑↓↑   ↓ ↑↓↑

5   Molla – moolla –
       r   /
             molla – moolla,
               r   /
     Molla – moolla –
       r   /
             molla – moolla:
               r   /

2   Hold your fists up at about chest height, next to each other. The edges of your pinkies are facing towards the children. At each "poom," bounce your fists against each other. At "pah," bounce your fists once more against each other and then swing them up sideways above your head, almost stretching your arms. Call the "pah" slowly; be sure to take enough time. Repeat the movements again.

3   As in 1.

4   At the syllable "hop," bounce your fists on your thighs. Bounce them up to your face, then back onto your thighs, bouncing them at "la" only as high as your stomach. The movement accents the syllable "pa," as does your use of a higher tone while speaking.

5   As in 1.

connection with themselves by bouncing their fists against the chest. Lastly, there is an awakening gesture during "whoops!" while throwing up one's arms in an awakening gesture.

6   Pom – pom – peck!
    Pom – pom – pawn!

6   Bounce your fists against your chest at "pom." At "peck" and "pawn," hold your left fist forward and cover it with your flat right hand.

7   Molla – moolla –
        r   /
            molla – moolla,
                r   /
    Molla – moolla –
        r   /
            molla – moolla:
                r   /

7   As in 1.

8   Whoops! And gone!

8   At "whoops," swing your fists above your head and then in a great arc behind your back so that at "gone" they have disappeared.

9   All gone!

9   The game may be repeated two or three times. At the final ending, show both open hands to the children. See, Molla and Moolla have gone!

Croll and Crooll
Hand Movement Game for Fists

Croll and Crooll
Wind the wool,
Wind-a-wind a ball of wool.
Rolla-rolla, wind a big ball of wool.
Rolla-rolla, wind an enormous ball of wool!
    E – nor – mous!

Then Croll and Crooll
Give the ball of wool a push!
It rolls – rolls – rolls,
    Trolls – trolls – trolls
        Far – far – away.

Croll and Crooll look on and on —
Can't see where the ball has gone. —

Yet the end of the thread
Still lies nearby.
Says Croll to Crooll:
"We'll get it if we try!"

Croll and Crooll
Wind the wool,
Wind-a-wind a ball of wool.
Rolla-rolla, wind a big ball of wool.
Rolla-rolla, wind an enormous ball of wool!
    E – nor – mous!

    They've got it back
        And are shouting for joy: "Ut hoy! – Ut hoy!"

Croll and Crooll
Put the ball of wool into the chest.
They shut the lid,
And take a rest.

TEXT:	GESTURES:
1 *Silent*	1 Silently, make both hands into loose fists; your thumbs lie on top of your pointers. Both fists rest on your thighs on the edges of your pinkies. Silently lift both fists to about stomach height. The backs of your fists face the children.
2 Croll and Crooll *r* *l*	2 Croll and Crooll are introduced by inclining first your right fist (Croll), then your left fist (Crooll) toward the children, then returning them to their previous positions.

3 Wind the wool,
    r   *l*
  up   *up*
	3 Turn your fists slowly around each other in narrow circles, beginning with you right fist on top and outward, in a flowing movement. The speech rhythm must correspond with the movement.

4 Wind-a-wind a ball
    r   *l*   *r*
  up *up* *up*
           of wool.
             l
            up
	4 Continue winding as for 3, with your right fist again on top. To begin with, the children will wind in a free rhythm. This is fine and must not be corrected.

5 Rolla-rolla, wind a
    r *l* *r* *l*
       big ball of wool.
        r *l*   *r*
	5 Continue as in 3, but increase the width of the circles you are winding, but not too big, so that there is still room for increase at "enormous." Adjust the speed of your speech to your movements.

6 Rolla-rolla, wind an
       r   /   *r*   /
      enormous ball of wool!
           r   /   *r*

6 Continue as in 3. The circles increase again and the speech tempo slows accordingly. The last circle is as large as possible, but don't overstretch. Movement must be controlled.

7 E – nor – mous!

7 Short pause. Move your hands upward, showing the big ball by forming a large circle. Move your open hands outward as if sliding along the ball's circumference. At the bottom, hold your hands next to each other, with palms up.

8 Then Croll and Crooll
9 Give the ball of wool a

8 As in 1 and 2.
9 At the same time move both fists back, and to the right and left of your head, bending your upper body back, ready for a push.

10 push!
    ↑↑

10 With both fists, push quickly and firmly forward, moving along with your upper body.

11 It rolls – rolls – rolls,
     r   /   *r*
12 Trolls – trolls – trolls
    /   *r*   /

11 As in 3.

12 Open your hands and alternately move them away from yourself. Start with your left hand in a rolling movement. Each hand reaches a little further. Move your upper body along.

13 Far – far – away.
     r   /   *r*

13 Continue as in 12, with your hands and upper body pointing further forward. At the same time, your movement and speech slow.

14	*silent*	14	For a little while, stay bent forward looking after the ball. Then straighten out, forming your fists as Croll and Crooll.
15	Croll and Crooll	15	As in 2.
	r l		
16	look on and on - - -	16	Hold both hands against your forehead like a visor, looking after the ball.

17	*silent*	17	Keeping the same gesture, seek to the left, then to the right.
18	Can't see where the ball has gone. —	18	Shake your head slightly, dropping your hands.
19	Yet —	19	Lift both hands with your pointers stretched.
20	the end of the thread still lies near by.	20	Point downward with your forefingers from the up position in a slow movement. The movement should take as long as the words. Only then have the fingertips arrived down.
21	*silent*	21	As in 1.
22	Says Croll to Crooll:	22	First the right fist (Croll) bends sideways to the left fist (Crooll), then the left fist to the right fist, each time calling their names.
	r l		
23	"We'll get it if we try!"	23	Move both fists forward and down, then back to their previous positions, as if they picked something up.

24 Croll and Crooll
　　Wind the wool,
　　Wind-a-wind a ball of wool.
　　Rolla-rolla, wind a
　　　　big ball of wool.
　　Rolla-rolla, wind an
　　　　enormous ball of wool!
　　E – nor – mous!

24 As in 2 to 7.

25 They've got it back

25 Two possibilities:
　　a) Hold the "enormous ball" at its sides and, bending a little forward, show it to the children.
　　b) Surround the enormous ball with both arms until your fingertips touch.

26 And are shouting for joy:
　　　　"Ut hoy! – Ut hoy!"
　　　　o　o　　o　o

26 Lift your hands upright, palms outward on "o," and turn them in and out in a lively way.

27 Croll and Crooll
　　　r　　　l

27 As in 2.

28 Put the ball of wool
　　　　　　into the chest.

28 Grasp the big, imaginary ball at right and left with both hands and lay it with a little bounce before your feet (chest).

29 They shut the lid,

29 Rest both hands, palms down, as a "lid" on the imaginary chest. Stay like that for a short while.

30 And take a rest.

30 Straighten up, and at "rest" fold your arms and remain sitting for a while. Then you can sing or hum a lullaby, rocking lightly with your upper body in the rhythm of the song.

Pum and Pom

Small Rhythmic Story for Fists

Pum and Pom, each brother
Is fond of the other.

Pum and Pom, they walk together:
Walk – walk – walk – walk,
Into the world they walk.

Turn around and walk together:
Walk – walk – walk – walk,
Back, back home they walk.
And from their quest they rest.

They're jumping now; just see how.
Pum over Pom, Pom over Pum,
Pum over Pom, Pom over Pum,
Pum – Pom – Pum – Pom,
Hop – hop – hop – and stop!
Now once again, to and fro,
Pum and Pom jump no mo'e.

They're climbing now; just see how.
Pum on Pom, Pom on Pum,
Pum on Pom, Pom on Pum,
Pum – Pom – Pum – Pom,
Higher – higher – way up high.
Oh, my!
They sit there dizzily,
All fearfully.
Thud!
They lie in the mud!
Pum and Pom do not stay,
They run – run – run away!

TEXT:	MOVEMENTS:
1 Pum and Pom, 	1 Form loose fists. Your thumbs lie on your fingers with the edges of your pinkies on the bottom. "Pum" is your right fist, "Pom" your left fist. As you call their names, set your right fist on your right thigh, your left fist on your left thigh.
2 each brother	2 Lift both fists a little: Pum and Pom are introduced.
3 Is fond of the other.	3 Just above your thighs, move your fists toward each other; at "fond," press against each other tenderly.

4 Pum and Pom, they
    r   /
        walk together:
          r   /
Walk – walk –
  r   /
        walk – walk,
      r   /
Into the world they walk – .
  r   /   *r* /
	4 Taking turns, both fists walk together along your thighs toward your knees. Carefully adjust the movement so that they arrive at your knees at the last "walk." Start with your right fist. Rhythmic speaking and light, bouncy movement must fit together. The last step is taken without an accompanying word.

5 Turn around and
    r   /
        walk together:
          r   /
Walk – walk –
  r   /
        walk – walk,
      r   /
Back, back home
  r   /
        they walk – .
         r /
	5 Taking turns, both fists walk rhythmically back from your knees to your upper body.

6 And from their quest
                    they rest.

7 They're jumping now; just
                    see how.

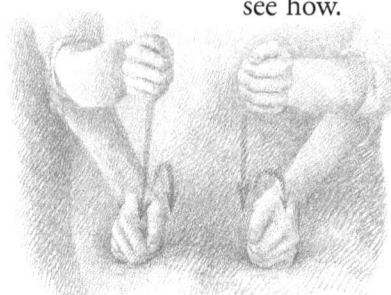

8 Pum over Pom,

        Pom over Pum,

  Pum over Pom,

        Pom over Pum,

  Pum – Pom – Pum – Pom,

  Hop – hop – hop –

                and stop!

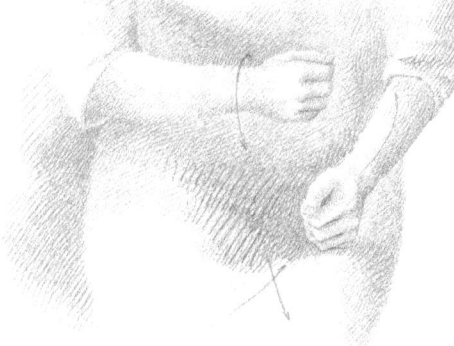

9 Now once again, to
                    and fro,
  Pum and Pom jump
                    no mo'e.

6 Turn both fists so that they lie on your thighs with the rolled-up fingers down. Take a brief pause.

7 At "they're," tip your fists back on the edges of your pinkies. At "jumping," and "just," both fists bounce up. After the second jump, your fists come down one behind the other, your right fist closer to your body, your left fist closer to your knee.

8 Your right fist now jumps over your left fist to a position closer to your knee. While your right fist jumps, withdraw your left fist to the empty spot from which your right fist just came. Now your left fist jumps over your right fist as your right fist is withdrawn so that the jumping will always happen at the same place on your thighs. At the last "and," quickly raise your right fist, keeping it raised. This puts a stop to the movement. At "stop," set down both fists on your lap keeping them still for a while. The jumping must be light and bouncy. The speed picks up, but remains rhythmically controlled until the end.

9 At "to," jump once more with both fists in the direction of your knees and at "fro," arch back to their former position. Hold both

10 They're climbing now;
    ↑   ↑
            just see how.

11 Pum on Pom, Pom on Pum,
        o   o
    Pum on Pom, Pom on Pum,
        o   o
    Pum – Pom – Pum – Pom,
     o   o   o   o
    Higher – higher – way
       o   o   o   o
                up high.
                 o o

12 Oh, my!

13 They sit there dizzily,

fists still, looking at them. When calling their names, turn your right fist (Pum), then your left fist (Pom), and lay them on your thighs on the rolled-up fingers. At "no mo'e," shake your head no.

10 Turn both fists back onto the edges of your pinkies and, with rolled-in fingers facing each other, move them up together. Speak slowly, stretching the words. After the text line is finished return both fists to your thighs.

11 At "o," put your left fist on top of your right fist, still on your thigh. Then, at the next "o," pull out your right fist from under your left fist, without moving the position of your left fist, and set it on top. Do the same with your left fist, leaving the position of your right fist intact. This way your fists climb up rhythmically. The higher they climb, the slower the movement. One can see the "effort." The tone of your speech also rises and becomes louder. Be careful not to overstretch your arms!

12 At "Oh, my," swing your fists (one on top of the other) back over your head.

13 At "dizzily," swing forwards toward the children.

Overstretching your arms has the effect of turning the game from a hand-movement game into a large-movement, whole body game. The children will then impulsively climb on their chairs and jump or pretend to fall down.

14 All fearfully.

15 Thud!
  ↓ ↓

16 They lie in the mud!

17 Pum and Pom do not stay,
   r   l

18 They run – run – run away!

14 At "fearfully," swing again back, then silently again forward, and then suddenly:

15 Drop both fists, with rolled-in fingers facing downward, onto your thighs, bouncing them slightly. Stop in this position a while.

16 Look at your fists and at the words "lie," and "mud," nod your head.

17 When naming the fists, tip each back on the edge of your pinkies.

18 Both fists run quickly behind your back, one on each side.

GROUP 2: GAMES FOR THUMBS AND FINGERS

Tom and Tim

Thumb Game with Sound Syllables

TOM AND TIM:
TIP – TOP – TIP – TOP – TIP – TOP – TIP – TOP.
TOM AND TIM:
WIP – WOP – WIP – WOP – WIP – WOP – WIP – WOP.
TOM AND TIM:
NIMA – NIMA – NIMANIMA – NOP!
TOM AND TIM:
SNIP – SNOP – SNIP – SNOP – SNIP – SNOP – SNIP –
AND SNOP!

TEXT:

1 Tom and Tim:

2 Tip – top – tip – top –
    r   /   r   /
    tip – top – tip – top.
    r   /   r   /

MOVEMENTS:

1 Quietly form fists with both of your hands, thumbs inside your fists, and set them half way on your thighs onto the edges of your pinkies. Now Tom and Tim will be introduced. First lift your right fist, and, as you name it, stick out your thumb. Do the same with "Tim." Pause. Hold your fists down a little above your thighs.

2 First lower your right thumb onto your rolled-in pointer, then lower your left thumb onto your left pointer. As your one thumb is lowered, your other thumb is lifted. So, in turn, move your thumbs four times up and down in fast rhythm. After the last time both thumbs remain lying for a while.

The thumb is the will area of your hand. This game stresses the experience of space, of down – up, inside – outside, round – straight, front – back. The text shows a constant change of m to p, and from o to i and from i to o. Also there is a rhythmic change from joy of movement to control of movement with self-touch.

3   Tom and Tim:
4   Wip – wop – wip – wop –
       X   v   X   v
    wip – wop – wip – wop.
       X   v   X   v

3   As in 1.
4   Hold both fists with rolled-in fingers in front of you a little above your thighs. Cross your thumbs at "wip." At "wop," move your thumbs apart to right and left. After the last time, lower your thumbs onto your rolled-in pointers and rest a little while.

5   Tom and Tim:
6   Nima – nima – nimanima – nop!

5   As in 1.
6   Hold both fists with rolled-in pointers a little above your thighs. Your thumbs are stretched horizontally toward each other. Then turn your thumbs around each other in free speech rhythm. At "nop," turn your fists up so that the pinkie edges face down. Lay your thumbs on your pointers for a short while, then stretch them up again.

7   Tom and Tim:
8   Snip – snop – snip –
       ↓↑   ↑↓   ↓↑
     snop – snip – snop –
       ↑↓   ↓↑   ↑↓
            snip –
             ↓↑

7   As in 1.
8   Rhythmically move your thumbs in opposite directions forward and backward so that they touch each other. The movement should be small and fast. Start slapping with your right thumb against your left thumb.

9 And snop!

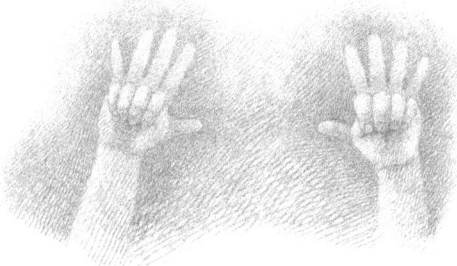

10 *Silent*

9 At "and," open your fists very slowly until your fingers are all stretched toward the children. At the same time your thumbs are directed against each other. Speak very slowly. Watch your movements and especially those of your thumbs very closely. At "snop," cover your thumbs with the fingers of both of your hands. Don't move too abruptly.

10 Cross your arms, letting your fists with the "snopped" thumbs disappear under your armpits. Sit like that for a bit, then dissolve the gesture.

Boomsti! – Woomsti!

Rhythmic Syllable Game for Thumbs

Boomsti! Woomsti!
Boolli – boolli – boolli – boolli – bop!

Boomsti! Woomsti!
Woolli – woolli – woolli – woolli – wop!

Boomsti! Woomsti!
Boomsti! Woomsti!
Boomsti – woomsti – bup!

Boomsti! Woomsti!
Boolli – boolli – woolli – woolli – wup!

TEXT:	MOVEMENTS:	PRONUNCIATION:
1 Boomsti!	1 Form your hands into fists; your thumbs are enclosed by your fingers. Stand them on the pinky edge on your thighs. When calling "Boomsti," slightly raise your right fist and, at the sound of "B," poke your thumb straight up from your fist.	"oo" in Boomsti pronounced short, as in "brook."
2 Woomsti!	2 Slightly raise your left fist and, at the sound of "W," poke your left thumb straight up from your fist.	

3 Boolli – boolli – boolli –
   r l   r l   r l
                boolli
                 r l
	3 Turn your fists with the protruding thumbs so that the back of your hands are up and the front joints of your thumbs lie one in front of the other. At "boolli - booli," rhythmically turn your thumbs around each other as in "twiddling your thumbs." At the syllable	

35

4	Bop!	4	"boo," your right thumb always moves downwards in front of your left thumb, and at "li," your left thumb moves in the same way.

4 Bop!
                    4 After the last turn, separate your thumbs a little to the right and left. Exactly at "bop," your two thumb tips touch, lightly pressing against each other.

5 Boomsti!   5 When calling its name, turn your right fist so that the thumb pokes back up.

6 Woomsti!   6 Turn your left fist so that the thumb pokes up.

7 Woolli – woolli – woolli –
    r l   *r l*   *r l*
                  woolli
                    r l   7 As in 3.

8 wop!   8 At the syllable "wop," turn your fists down so that the thumb tips stand on your thighs close to your knees.

9 Boomsti! Woomsti!
   forward   *back*
   Boomsti! Woomsti!
   forward   *back*
   Boomsti – woomsti –
   forward   *back*   9 While holding this position, rhythmically rock your upper body back and forth. The movement starts very small, increasing in size. The sound of your voice increases together with the size of the movement.

10 bup!   10 Together with the syllable "bup," turn your fists quickly so that your thumbs stand up again.

11 Boomsti!   11 When calling the name of the right fist, move it a little toward the participants.

12 Woomsti!   12 Your left fist repeats the movement of 11.

13 Boolli – boolli – woolli – woolli –

14 wup!

13 Movement as in 3.

14 Together with the syllable "wup," both thumbs disappear into their fists. Look at your fists, then look happily at the children. Relax your hands and let them hang down.

Flip and Flop I
Rhythmic Game for Thumbs

Flip and Flop
They dance and sing
In a joyous round-a-ring.
Round-a-ring, round-a-ring,
Flip and Flop now dance and sing.

Flip and Flop
Now wad-dle, wad-dle
To and fro, to and fro,
Wad-dle, wad-dle,
And they waddle now no more.

Flip and Flop
Are jumping:
Hoppsa-hop! Hoppsa-hop
Jumping jumping
Flip and Flop.

Now they bow, each one,
Slip into their house (bed)
And the game is done.

TEXT:		MOVEMENTS:	
1	Flip and Flop	1	Form fists; your thumbs are enclosed by your fingers. Set your thumbs on your thighs on the edges of your pinkies. "Flip" and "Flop" are introduced by sticking up your right thumb at "Flip" and your left thumb by "Flop." Raise both fists with their thumbs sticking out toward each other until both fists touch.

2   They dance and sing
          o   o

3   In a joyous round-a-ring.
    o ↑ ↑   o   o

4   Round-a-ring, round-a-ring,
    o   o   o   o
    Flip and Flop now
    o   o
            dance and sing.
              o   o

5   Flip and Flop
    /   /

6   Now wad-dle, wad-dle
    ←   →   ←   →

    To and fro, to and fro,
    ←   →   ←   →

    Wad-dle, wad-dle,
    ←   →   ←   →

    And they waddle
    ←   →
                now no more.
              ↑↑   ↓↓

2   Your thumbs circle against each other in rhythm with the speech. The circling of both thumbs begins in the middle with a little jump backwards. Then your thumbs part to right and left outside, then approach each other again in the front and come together again in the middle. Continue this movement.

3   While circling both thumbs make a little jump at "joyous."

4   Your thumbs continue dancing. Then end the dance with a little pause.

5   At "Flip," briefly touch your right pointer with your right thumb, and correspondingly move your left thumb at "Flop."

6   Rhythmically, as shown, continue your parallel thumbs left, then right, to and fro. At "no," straighten your thumbs and raise them lightly. By "more," return your fists, with thumbs sticking up, to their starting point on your thighs. Hold still for a while.

7 Flip and Flop
8 Are jumping:
   ↑↑ ↓↓
   Hoppsa-hop! Hoppsa-hop
   ↑↑ ↓↓ ↑↑ ↓↓
   Jumping jumping
   ↑↑   ↓↓
   Flip and Flop.
   ↑↑   ↓↓
9 Now they bow, each one,
10 Slip into their house (bed)

11 And the game is done.

7 Same as 5.
8 At "jumping," move both fists rhythmically with your thumbs outstretched up and down. After touching down on your thighs, bounce your fists up once as the beginning of the next jump.
9 Same as 5.
10 By "slip," hide both thumbs inside their fists.
11 Open both fists and show your empty hands, palms up, to the children.

Flip and Flop II
Rhythmic Movement Game

FIRST WE GO AROUND THE RING
AND DANCE A JOYOUS ROUND-A-RING.

Quietly Circling   TEXT AND MELODY: WILMA ELLERSIEK

ROUND-A-RING, ROUND-A-RING, WE ARE DANC-ING ROUND-A-RING.

ROUND-A-RING, ROUND-A-RING, IN A JOY-OUS ROUND-A-RING.

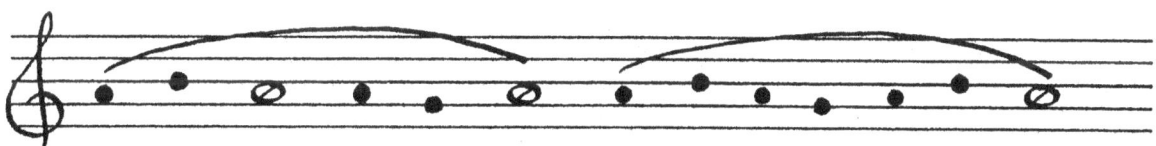

ROUND-A-RING, ROUND-A-RING, LIKE FLIP AND FLOP A-ROUND-A-RING.

NOTATION • ≈ ONE PULSATION IN MIDDLE TEMPO (BASIC UNIT) |⌀ ≈ •• |
o ≈ •••• / ⌢ ≈ ONE BREATH

EACH CHILD FOR THE ROUND-A-RING
TAKES PARTNER NOW TO DANCE AND SING,
AND DANCE WITH HIM IN ROUND-A-RING,
IN A JOYOUS ROUND-A-RING.

FLIP AND FLOP NOW WADDLE.

We waddle, waddle, to and fro, to and fro.
Like Flip and Flop, we waddle, waddle
To and fro, to and fro, and: no more.

Flip and Flop are jumping.

Hoppsa-hop! Hoppsa-hop!
We're jumping now like Flip and Flop.
Hoppsa-hop! Hoppsa-hop!
Hoppsa-hop! Like Flip and Flop.

Flip and Flop are bowing down.

We're bowing down, bowing down
Like Flip and Flop, bowing down,
And stop!

Flip and Flop slip into their house.

We slip into our house –
Yoo-hoo!*

(And the game is done.**)

TEXT:	MOVEMENTS:	
1 First we go around the ring And dance a joyous round-a-ring.	1 Children and adults form a circle, holding hands.	
2 *Sing* Round-a-ring, round-a-ring, We are dancing round round-a-ring, Round-a-ring, round-a-ring, in a joyous round-a-ring. Round-a-ring, round-a-ring, like Flip and Flop a-round-a-ring,	2 All sing and dance round- a-ring. If the group is not able to do this, one can walk clockwise in a circle, one behind the next, your right shoulder towards the middle.	Stop at the end of the song. Then speak the words in 3.

3 Each child for the
              round-a-ring
   Takes partner now to
              dance and sing,
   And dance with him
              in round-a-ring,
   In a joysous round-a-ring.

4 *Repeat song*
   Round-a-ring, round-a-ring,
   We are dancing round
              round-a-ring,
   Round-a-ring, round-a-ring,
   in a joyous round-a-ring.
   Round-a-ring, round-a-ring,
   like Flip and Flop
              a-round-a-ring,

5 Flip and Flop now waddle:
   We wad-dle, wad-dle,
   ← → ← →
        to and fro, to and fro.
        ← → ← →
   Like Flip and Flop,
        ← →
        we wad-dle, wad-dle
        ← → ← →
   To and fro, to and fro,
   ← → ← →
              and: no more.

6 Flip and Flop are jumping!
   Hoppsa-hop! Hoppsa-hop!
      ↑↑   ↑↑
   We're jumping now like
        ↑↑
           Flip and Flop.
           ↑↑
   Hoppsa-hop! Hoppsa-hop!
      ↑↑   ↑↑
   Hoppsa-hop!
      ↑↑
           Like Flip and Flop.
           ↑↑

3 Each child takes a partner to dance round-a-ring together.

4 Repeat song as in 2.

5 Each child waddles alone in his/her place. To waddle, shift your weight from one leg to the other.

6 Jump with both feet together, first in place, then a little forward. After each jump land lightly and elasticly, before jumping again. Support each jump with your arms swinging.

7   Flip and Flop are
               bowing down!
We're bowing down,
               bowing down
Like Flip and Flop,
        we are bowing down,
And stop!

8   Flip and Flop slip
               into their house!
We slip into our house –
* Yoo-hoo!

7   Take lots of time for the bowing, perhaps you can turn to your neighbor and bow. Bow four times. In between: silently straighten up. End by: stop. Stand quietly for a moment.

8   Sit down on a stool or crouch down where you stand, circling your head with your arms. Stay a while this way. After "Yoo-hoo!" the game may be repeated. Alternately, you can remain seated and insert a rest with the words:
Flip and Flop, they rest now, too.
I sing (blow the flute, hum) for them a diddledoo.

Alternate Ending
9   ** And the game is done.

9   When you are ready to end the game, instead of "Yoohoo!" get up, spread your arms, showing empty hands. The game is done.

Pips and Pops
Rhythmic-Musical Story for Pointers

I'll tell you a story now.
Pips and Pops are making a joke,
Making a joke, listen how.

They bend down low, are pressing so,
Are pressing so.
Pull to and fro – to and fro.
Oooh! Ououou!
Ooff!
It doesn't go! It doesn't go!
Whoops! Whoosh!
They're sitting on their toosh!
Haw! You
Clumsy you, clumsy you!
You clumsy you!

To build a bridge they try,
And through the crack peep I!

TEXT:	MOVEMENTS:	PRONUNCIATION:
1 I'll tell you a story now.	1 Look cheerfully at the children.	Oooh! as in long Ououou! as in through Ooff! as in look
2 Pips and Pops 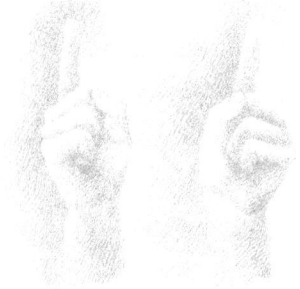	2 Introduce Pips and Pops: stick up right pointer (Pips), then stick up left pointer (Pops). Your other fingers are rolled up with thumbs on top. Hold awhile at about chin height.	
3 are making a joke, · · Making a joke, listen how! · · · ·	3 At the same time, tip both pointers lightly forward. Movement originates in your wrist. Next, tip twice to the left, then twice to the right. Move together with the speech rhythm.	

4   They bend down low,

5   are pressing so,
    → ← ← →

    Are pressing so.
    → ← ← →

6   Pull to and fro – to and fro.
    →   ←   →   ←

7   Oooh! Ououou!
    ← → → ←

    Ooff!
    ← →

8   It doesn't go!
         ↑   ↓

    It doesn't go!
         ↑   ↓

4   Turn your pointers toward each other. Pips and Pops look at each other. Slowly bend your pointers, stretching your words.

5   Press your bent pointers strongly together at their middle sections, stretching your words. At "so," separate slightly.

6   Hook your pointers together and pull them to the right, then to the left. Your right and then your left pointer pulls. At the second time, speak and move more slowly.

7   At the same time, your two hooked pointers pull against each other. Speak a slow "oooh" and "ouou," accompanying the failed effort to pull the one or the other to the other side. Don't moan realistically! At the third time pull against each other shortly but intensively.

8   While still pulling against each other, move your pointers up and down rhythmically. During the second time the hooking becomes more and more undone.

9 Whoops!

10 Whoosh!
    Look silently

11 They're sitting on
                their toosh!

12 Haw!

13 You,

14 *silent*

15 Clumsy you, clumsy you!

9   With a surprised call: "whoops," your pointers suddenly let go. Your hands fly up, pointers stretched, then at "whoosh," fall down as fists.

10 They land on your thighs with a small bounce. Don't hit too hard. Pips and Pops lost their balance when they let go, and fell down. First look silently at the two, then say the next line.

11 Nod your head twice. Then turn to the children and laugh. Give the children a chance to laugh, too, but not too long.

12 Stick out your pointers again and turn them towards each other. They are lying a distance apart. Pips and Pops look up.

13 Slowly move your pointers to their former play height. Pips and Pops are getting up.

14 Pips and Pops silently face each other.

15 Now beat down your pointers four times energetically, in the speech rhythm. They are approaching each other until they almost touch.

16 *silent*

16 For a moment, the two face each other very closely, then they silently move away from each other up to your shoulders. There they stop and look at each other from a distance. Watch these movements attentively as you perform them.

17 You clumsy you!

silent

17 Beat down with your pointers twice more, at a slower pace. Stick your pointers up again.

18 To build a bridge they try,

18 Move your pointer tips towards each other, and at "bridge," touch to form an arc.

19 And through the
        crack peep I!

19 Touch your thumb tips together as well, then look with your right eye through the peep hole you've created. Smile at the children.

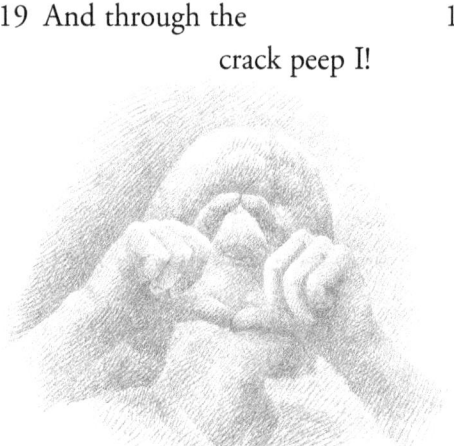

Bala Bane

Bala Bane, on toes goes he,
On his toes, so quietly –
Can you see? Can you see?

Bala Bane, on balls does hop.
Hear him pop? Hear him pop?

Bala Bane, on heels is stamping.
Hear him tramp – tramp – tramping?

On balls does hop, balls does hop!
Hear him pop? Hear him pop?

Heels are stamping, heels are stamping.
Hear him tramp – tramp – tramping?

On his toes, on toes goes he –
Softly, softly, can you see?

Bala Bane, now home must go –
Softly, softly on his toes,

Softly, softly, softly, softly,
Not a sign of him does show.

TEXT:

1   Bala Bane, on toes goes he –
    x   x   x   x
    P   M   P   M

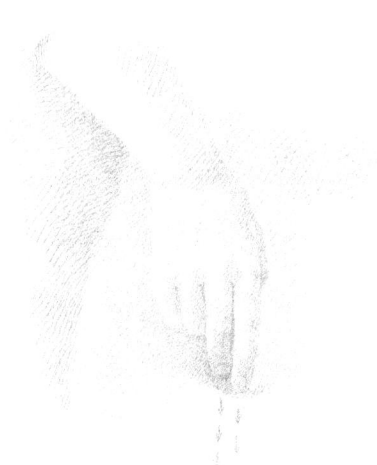

MOVEMENTS:

1   Your right hand appears from the back, walking (*x*) forward to your right knee on the fingertips of your pointer (*P*) and middle finger (*M*) in rhythmic speech.

On his toes, so quietly.

   x   x   x x
   P   M   P M

Can you see? Can you see?

   x   x x   x
   P   M P   M

2 Bala Bane, on balls
       •   •
              does hop
  Hear him pop?
      •
             Hear him pop?
                  •

2 Form a fist with your right hand. Fingers are rolled in and face down to your thighs. On the side, your thumb touches your pointer. Bounce your fist in rhythm (•) on your right thigh — not too hard, but bouncy. Meanwhile, your left hand rests lightly on your left thigh.

3 Bala Bane, on heels
       /   /
             is stamping.
  Hear him tramp –
      /
           tramp – tramping?
          /   /

3 Your right hand remains as a fist and hits (/) against your thigh with the ball of your hand. Since this movement is a bit more complicated, the younger children, perhaps, might hit their thighs with their fists against the sides of their pinkies. Allow this and don't correct them.

4 On balls does hop,
     •   •
           balls does hop!
          •   •
  Hear him pop?
    •   •
           Hear him pop?
           •   •

4 As in 2.

5 Heels are stamping,
  /
      heels are stamping.
         /
  Hear him tramp –
       /
      tramp – tramping?
        /   /

6 On his toes,
      x
      P
         on toes goes he –
             x
             M
  Softly, softly, can you see?
    x   x   x   x
    P   M   P   M

7 Bala Bane, now home
    x   x   x
    P   M   P
            must go—
               x
               M
  Softly, softly on his toes,
    x   x   x   x
    P   M   P   M

8 Softly, softly, softly, softly,
    x   x   x   x
    P   M   P   M

9 Not a sign of him
            does show.

5 As in 3. Not too hard and fast; the movements must be controlled.

6 The change from the very lively and loud movement to one that is soft and cautious must be well guided so that all children become calm again. Speaking slowly move your fingertips as in 1. Then, at "softly," in the same position, four times in turn lift and set them down to rhythmic speaking.

7 Walk along your thigh to the rhythmic speech, but backward from your knee to your upper body. Start with your pointer.

8 Your fingers disappear around your body and behind your back. Watch them move.

9 After a brief pause, turn to the children. Spread out your arms with open hands and shake your head.

Nicky

Rhythmic-Musical Game for your Pinky

Nicky is a plucky wight.
He takes no fright.
Tiny little peep
All alone will creep
In the dark hole deep.

"Hoo-hoo! – Boo-boo?"
"Hoo-hoo! – Boo-boo?"

Crawls out.
Haah! He's back, hurrah!
Nicky calls: "Brothers, go away."
"Go a-wa-ay!"
Goes: "Tickle – tickle – tick!"
"Tickle – tickle – tick!"
Doops! – Runs away quick!
Quick!

TEXT:	FINGER MOVEMENTS:
1 Nicky is a plucky wight. • •	1 Make a fist with your right hand, with your thumb on top of your rolled-in fingers. Your rolled-in fingers face the children. At the name: "Nicky," with special emphasis, stick your pinky straight up from your fist and at each " • ," tip twice forward into the air.
2 He takes no fright.	2 Shake your fist with the pinky sticking out to and fro as if shaking your head: "no."

52

3   Tiny little peep

3   Bring your fist close to your chest, turning it so that your thumb is turned toward you and your pinky toward the children. Hold your pinky slightly bent, to show how small he is. Before continuing with the poem, make a loose fist with your left hand, too, and rest it on your left thigh. Your thumb and pointer tips touch each other and form a hole.

4   All alone will creep

4   Move Nicky in an arc across and down to your left hand, nearing the hole.

5   In the dark hole deep.

5   Let Nicky creep into the hole as far as possible.

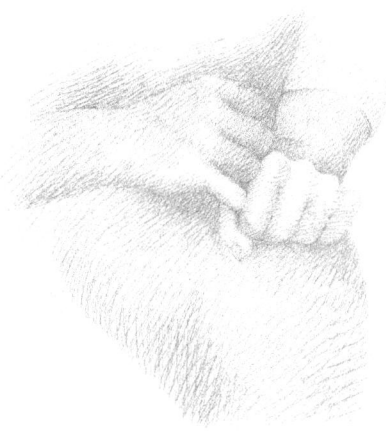

6   "Hoo-hoo! – Boo-boo?"

6   Nicky turns around in the hole while boldly calling a long, slow "hoo-hoo!" Then he calls in a deeper pitch the question: "boo-boo," raising his voice at the end. Speak in a slow and long manner, but not a dramatic way, so that the children don't get scared.

7   "Hoo-hoo! – Boo-boo?"

7   Repeat the calls of 6.

8	*silent*	8	Now Nicky holds himself very quiet in the hole. Bend a little forward as if listening.
9	Crawls out.	9	Slowly pull your pinky out of the hole.
10	Haah! He's back, hurrah!	10	Once Nicky is outside he stands again upright. First look at him with relief, then take a loud breath: "Haaah!" Energetically raise your pinky up to your head, holding him there as if to say: "look here!" and call in a light voice: "He's back! Hurrah!" Tip twice forward with your pinky as you speak.
11	*silent*	11	Turn over your left fist so that the back of your hand lies on your thigh. Your fingers are still rolled in with your fingernails facing upward.

12	Nicky calls: "Brothers,
	• •
	       go away."
	    • •
		12	With the tip of your pinky (Nicky), tap the nails of the fingers of your left hand (brothers) in the speech rhythm, (•). Start with the pinky of your left hand.

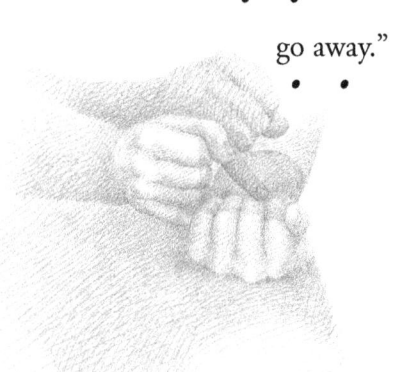

13	"Go a-wa-ay!"	13	Now stick the tip of your right pinky underneath the rolled-in fingers of your left hand and at: " a-wa-a-y," Press them up until your left hand is open and lies flat on your thigh.

14 Goes: "tickle – tickle – tick!"
  •   •   •
   "Tickle – tickle – tick!"
    •   •   •

15 Doops! – Runs away quick!
  •

16 Quick!

14 Nicky tickles rhythmically your left palm.

15 Nicky lightly taps the center of your palm, at (•), bounces back and stops briefly in midair. Then he disappears as you lay both your closed fists into your lap.

16 Both fists disappear behind your back as you call a light: "quick!"

Group 3: Games for Hands Alternating with Fingers

Oolla Woolla

Rhythmic-Musical Finger Game With Sound Syllables

Oolla – woolla – oolla – woolla
Oolla – woolla: Pack!

Oolla – woolla – oolla – woolla
Oolla – woolla: Snap!
Sits in the sack.

Pin – pun – pin – pun – pout.
Jumps out!

Hurray! Hurray!
He's back! Hurray!

Pin – pun – pin – pun – pay.
And away!

TEXT:

1   Oolla – woolla –
       r   /
              oolla – woolla
                r   /
    Oolla – woolla: Pack!
       r   /   •

MOVEMENTS:

1   Make fists with both hands. Your thumb lies on your pointer. Turn your fists around each other three times, starting with your right fist. At "pack," both hands grab each other heartily and hold tightly for a moment.

PRONUNCIATION: "Oo" short, as in "wool."

Young children like to repeat this game for a long time without change. Older children like to try new things. For example: they play loud and soft, slow and fast, or instead of the fists, they turn their thumbs or other fingers about each other.

57

2 Oolla – woolla –
        r   /
            oolla – woolla
                r   /
   Oolla – woolla: Snap!
        r   /   ↑

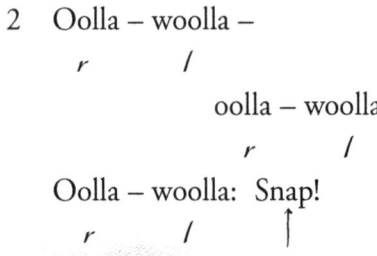

3 Sits in the sack.
   ♩ ♩   ♩

4 Pin – pun – pin – pun –
   ↑   ↓   ↑   ↓
          pout. Jumps out!
           ↑   ↓   ↗

5 Hurray! Hurray!
     ↷ ↶
          He's back! Hurray!
            ↷   ↶

2 Turn your fists three times as above. Then open your fists. Your right hand flies up, palm forward, then pushes down with your thumb extended. Your left hand comes toward it and at "snap," grabs your right thumb.

3 Your left hand tightly holds your right thumb. With your free fingers rhythmically wave forward three times. As you do this, your right, open palm is turned towards the children.

4 Your left hand continues to grab your right thumb. As you try to pull your thumb out, your left hand is pulled up. At "pun," your left hand pulls your thumb down again. This repeats rhythmically three times. At "out," your left hand releases your thumb. Move your right hand, thumb stretched out, in an upward arc.

5 Up above, rhythmically turn your fist in and out, with your thumb sticking out. Speak the "ay" in "hurray" slowly.

6   Pin – pun – pin –
              pun – pay.

6   Move your flat hands up and down facing each other, as with cymbals. When they meet, they make a clapping noise. Your right hand is first to move down.

7   And away!

7   Pause. At "and," make one more sounding clap as your left hand moves down. Then move both hands slowly backwards and at "away," they disappear behind your back.

So Play My Hands
Rhythmic-Musical Hand Game

So play my hands:
Tap-tap-tap-tap-tap.
So play my hands:
Clap-clap-clap-clap-clap.
They turn and turn and turn,
Stand firm.
Bend down low – and show.
Bend down low – and show.
Bye-bye-bye-bye-boh,
Bye-bye-bye-bye-boh,
Sinking, sinking low.

Play again:
Tap-tap-tap-tap-tap.
Clap-clap-clap-clap-clap.
They turn and turn and turn,
Stand firm.
Bend down low – and show.
Bend down low – and show.
Bye-bye-bye-bye-boh,
Bye-bye-bye-bye-boh,
Sinking, sinking low.

P LAY AGAIN:
T AP - TAP - TAP - TAP - TAP .
C LAP - CLAP - CLAP - CLAP - CLAP .
T HEY TURN AND TURN AND TURN ,
S TAND FIRM .
B END DOWN LOW – AND SHOW .
B END DOWN LOW – AND SHOW .
B YE - BYE - BYE - BYE - BOH ,
B YE - BYE - BYE - BYE - BOH ,
S INKING , SINKING LOW .

T HEY REST TOGETHER , EACH ONE ,
A ND THE GAME IS DONE .

TEXT:		MOVEMENTS:	
1	So play my hands:	1	Move both hands forward, fingers open, in a little arc toward the front. Show the children your open hands.

2	Tap-tap-tap-tap-tap. r / r / r	2	Move your hands back again in a small arc and slap your thighs rhythmically right and left.
3	So play my hands:	3	As in 1.
4	Clap-clap-clap-clap-clap. • • • • •	4	Move both of your hands back in an arc, and rhythmically clap them in front of you .

5   They turn and turn
         o   o   o
        in out in
                and turn,
                 o   o
                out in

5   Vertically lift your arms, with hands open, and rhythmically turn them in and out.

6   Stand firm.

6   Lower your hands so that they face each other, with your fingertips pointing upward. Speak slowly. Hold your hands like that for a short while.

7   Bend down low –
             and show.
    Bend down low –
             and show.

7   "Bend down low:" Bend your wrists smoothly toward each other. "Show:" Straighten your hands again, and with fingers spread, turn your hands forward and show them to the children. Do this twice.

8   Bye-bye-bye-bye-boh,
     ↑↓   ↑↓   ↑↓
    Bye-bye-bye-bye-boh,
     ↑↓   ↑↓   ↑↓

8   At "↑↓," move your open hands rhythmically up and down from your wrist. Stop shortly after the first line, then repeat it.

9   Sinking, sinking low.

9   Both hands sink down very slowly, with palms down and relaxed fingers, like little parachutes. At "low," rest your hands on your thighs. Take a brief pause.

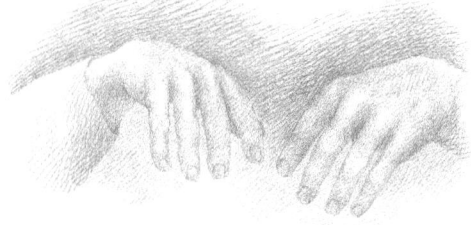

10 Play again:
   Tap-tap-tap-tap-tap.
   Clap-clap-clap-clap-clap.
   They turn and
           turn and turn,
   Stand firm.
   Bend down low –
           and show.
   Bend down low –
           and show.
   Bye-bye-bye-bye-boh,
   Bye-bye-bye-bye-boh,
   Sinking, sinking low.

11 Play again: *(silent)*

Ending:

12 They rest together,
           each one,

13 And the game is done.
       x   x

10 Lift up both hands and then repeat all movements from 2 to 9. Then relax.

11 Lift up both hands and then repeat all movements from 2 to 9 rhythmically, but without speaking the text. Take a brief pause.

12 After your hands have come to rest on your thighs, lay one hand into the other in your lap and rest this way for a little while.

13 Turn toward the children with a smile, speak calmly and nod your head twice. Your hands remain at rest.

Weedle Woodle
Rhythmic-Musical Hand Game

Weedle – woodle – weedle – woodle.
Diddle – doodle – diddle – doodle.

Binka – winka – binka – winka.
Kinka – linka – kinka – linka.

Onka – onka – ponka – ponka.
Onka – onka – paaaah!

Weedle – woodle – weedle – woodle.
Diddle – doodle – diddle – doodle.
Weedle – woodle – wout – – and out!

TEXT:

1   Weedle – woodle –
       O   O
            weedle – woodle.
               O   O
    Diddle – doodle –
       O   O
            diddle – doodle.
               O   O

2   Binka – winka –
       X   X
            binka – winka.
               X   X
    Kinka – linka –
       X   X
            kinka – linka.
               X   X

MOVEMENTS:

1   Lift both of your hands at the same time, with stretched fingers, to about head height and turn them in and out at the wrists with the speech rhythm. As you turn them inward, your pinkies look at each other, turning outward, your thumbs do the same. Begin by turning in.

2   With open hands, rhythmically and happily wave to the children by bending hands at wrists.

With very young children end the game here. Rest your hands on your thighs, then, smiling, bend forward to the child and speak in a singing voice: "Aaah!" or "Aye!"

3	Onka – onka – • • 　　ponka – ponka. 　　　• • Onka – onka – • •	3	Form your hands into loose fists, with rolled-in fingers facing downward. Your thumbs lie on top of your pointers. In the given speech rhythm, bounce with both fists together on your thighs, lightly and airily.
4	paaaah! • ↑↑	4	Bounce your fists once more, then let them jump up to head height. Call "paaah" slowly while opening your fists and stretching your fingers. Your palms are turned forward.
5	Weedle – woodle – o o 　　weedle – woodle. 　　　o o Diddle – doodle – o o 　　diddle – doodle. 　　　o o	5	As in 1.
6	Weedle – woodle – wout – o o → • • ←	6	Turn in and out once more, then at "wout," form fists, still at head height. Your thumbs lie loosely on your rolled-in fingers. Bring your fists down energetically, to about stomach height, holding them there next to each other for a little while.

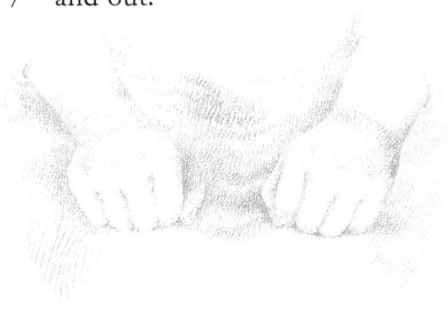

7	and out!	7	At "and," turn your fists, with rolled-in fingers facing downward, and at "out," quickly lay them on your thighs.

If you want to repeat the game start again after 7. For the final ending add 8. In this game the little child's basic gestures, which he or she already uses in the cradle, are employed. First is the turning of the lifted hands in "weedle-woodle."

65

8   *Ending:*
    and out.

8   Slowly and quietly move your fists behind your back. Almost sing the "and." At "out," your fists disappear behind your back, slowly, for this leads to rest. Nod at the children and smile.

For infants this is the expression of joy and dancing movement, as long as they cannot dance with their feet yet. With "binka-winka-kinka-linka," infants establish contact to another person. By beating their fists up and down, as in "onka-onka-ponka-ponka," they express intensive engagement with their surroundings. By lifting their arms and opening their hands at the same time as in "paah," they express joyous self-awareness.

Trip By Boat
Small Story with Hand Gestures

See, today, these many folk
Go a-journeying in a boat!
They embark:
Heave-ho! – Heave-ho!
Into the sea they row their skiff.
Phfffffff! – Phfffffff!
A storm blows up with a whiff!
Danger call – for the vessel small!
On the bounding waves it's rocking
Bouncing up – and down –
Teetering to – and fro –
Capsizes!
– – – –
Where are the folks?
Where could they be?
Two are poking out of the sea.
They turn – wh – wh - whupph! – the boat up.
Hurray! – Hurray!
All folks are back, I say!
Heave-ho! – Heave-ho!
Rowing home – the journey's done –
They debark,
And quickly, quickly home they run.

TEXT:		MOVEMENTS:	
1	See, today,	1	Lift both hands, palms towards the children, with fingers stretched up.
2	these many folk	2	Move all fingers lightly as the "folk".

3   Go a-journeying in a boat!

4   They embark:

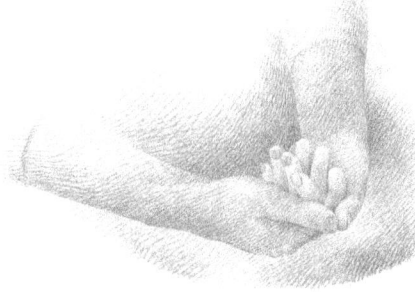

5   Heave-ho! – Heave-ho! –
    ↑ ↓   ↑ ↓
    Into the sea they
    ↑ ↓ ↑ ↓ ↑
              row their skiff.
              ↓ ↑ ↓

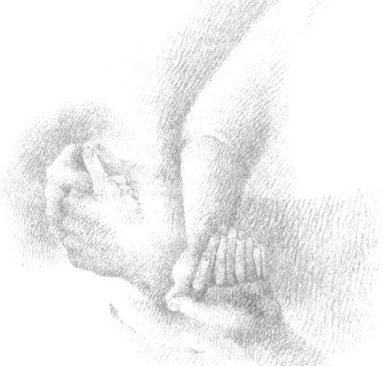

6   Phffffff! – Phffffff!
    ↑   ↓

7   A storm blows up with
    ↑
                    a Whiff!
                    ↓
    Danger call –
    ↑
              for the vessel small!
              ↓

3   Join your cupped hands on your thighs with the edges of your pinkies together and your thumbs on top of your pointers as "the boat."

4   Now turn your hands, palms still up, by 90 degrees until your middle fingertips touch each other. Slide your fingers into each other to the base of your fingers stretching them up. The folks are sitting in the boat. Your thumb tips touch in front.

5   Rhythmically move your hands held in the previous position (boat with folks.) Six small forward and backward movements show the rowing ("heave" = forward, "ho" = back). Close your fingers at "ho," as you move your hands back slightly. At the last time your hands are down just above your knees. The accent of speech and movement are always together. Accentuate this sentence very rhythmically.

6   Swing the "boat with the folks" up in a small, forward arc, then back again.

7   As in 6.

8 On the bounding waves ↑
          it's rocking ↓
9 Bouncing up – and down –
      ↑   ↓
10 Teetering to – and fro –
      ←   →

11 Capsizes!

12 – – – –
     ←   →
   (silent)
13 Where are the folks? ---
         ←
14 Where could they be? ---
         →
15 Two are poking out of
              the sea.

16 They turn – wh –
          wh - whupph! –
   the boat up.

17 Hurray! – Hurray!
   All folks are back, I say!

8 As in 6 but increase the arc.

9 As in 8.

10 In a wide arc, move the boat to the left at "to" and to the right at "fro."

11 Turn the boat over so that your fingers point down.

12 Silently swing the "capsized boat" first left, then right.

13 Swing the capsized boat to the left.

14 Swing the capsized boat to the right.

15 Hold the capsized boat in the middle in front of you. Your thumbs move in a lively way. At "two," poke up your thumbs. The boat remains capsized.

16 Rhythmically poke up your thumbs three times at "wh" until the boat stands vertically on the edges of your pinkies, and your knuckles face the children. Hold the boat a moment suspended; then, at "up," it returns to its former position. The folks look up again.

17 Move your fingers in a lively way as you place the boat back above your knees to give it enough room for the journey back.

18 Heave-ho! – Heave-ho!
   ↑ ↓ ↑ ↓
   Rowing home –
   ↑ ↓ ↑
   the journey's done –
   ↓ ↑ ↓ ↑ ↓
19 They debark,

20 And quickly, quickly
   P M P M
   home they run.
   P M P

18 As in 5, but now row toward your body. The "boat docks" when it reaches the tops of your thighs and rests there.
19 Slide your upright fingers apart to right and left.
20 Turn your hands, palms down. Rhythmically "walk" along your thighs with pointer and middle finger of both hands towards your body until the folks have disappeared behind your back. If necessary, continue "walking" until your fingers have totally disappeared behind your back.

Tompa-Tempa I
Call of the fifth, with hand gestures

TEXT:	MOVEMENTS:
1 Tompa-tempa! 　　　Tompa-tempa! 	1 Move your hands rhythmically in opposite directions: from top to bottom and bottom to top, clapping lightly as they pass each other, like cymbals.
2 Tom-pa-toooo! 	2 At the same time slap your thighs with both flat hands three times. Following the third slap, at "toooo," raise your loosely hanging hands slowly as if to pull them out of a sticky dough.
3 Tompa-tempa! 　　　Tompa-tempa!	3 As in 1.
4 Tom-pa-toooo!	4 As in 2.
5 Heh-heh-heh! 　　　Hel-le-le-le-leh! 	5 Stretch your hands up and rhythmically turn them from your wrists in a lively way. Allow yourself time for the next gesture.
6 Om-ba-om-ba! 　　　Om-ba-lom-ba!	6 Form fists with both of your hands. Your thumbs lie on your pointers. Hold your fists before you, at about stomach height. Hit your left fist with your right fist (in the speech rhythm.) Rock your fists to and fro as your do this.

This game is designed especially for children of three years and up. For older children, five years and up, you can extend the game by adding jingle sticks.

7 Om-ba-lom-ba-loh!

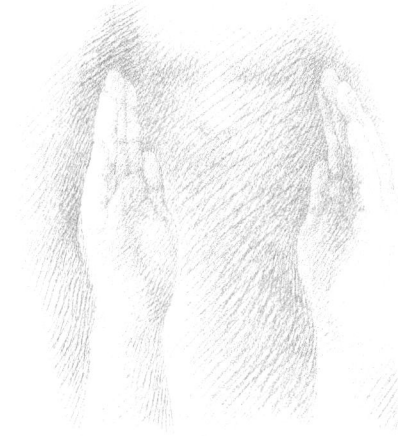

8 Omba-omba! Omba-lomba!
   Omba-lomba-loh!
9 Hol-la-hoh! Hol-la-hoh!
    o   o o o   o   o o o

10 *silent*

7 Twice more as in 6. At "loh," form a megaphone at your mouth with both hands and sing the long "oh."

8 As in 6 and 7.

9 Hold your hands above your head as in 5 and turn them loosely at the wrist in a lively way.

10 Lower your hands, from up down along the outside, drawing a large "*o*" into the air. Then rest your hands in your lap and remain sitting quietly for a short while.

Tompa-Tempa II
Call of the Fifth, with Jingle Stick

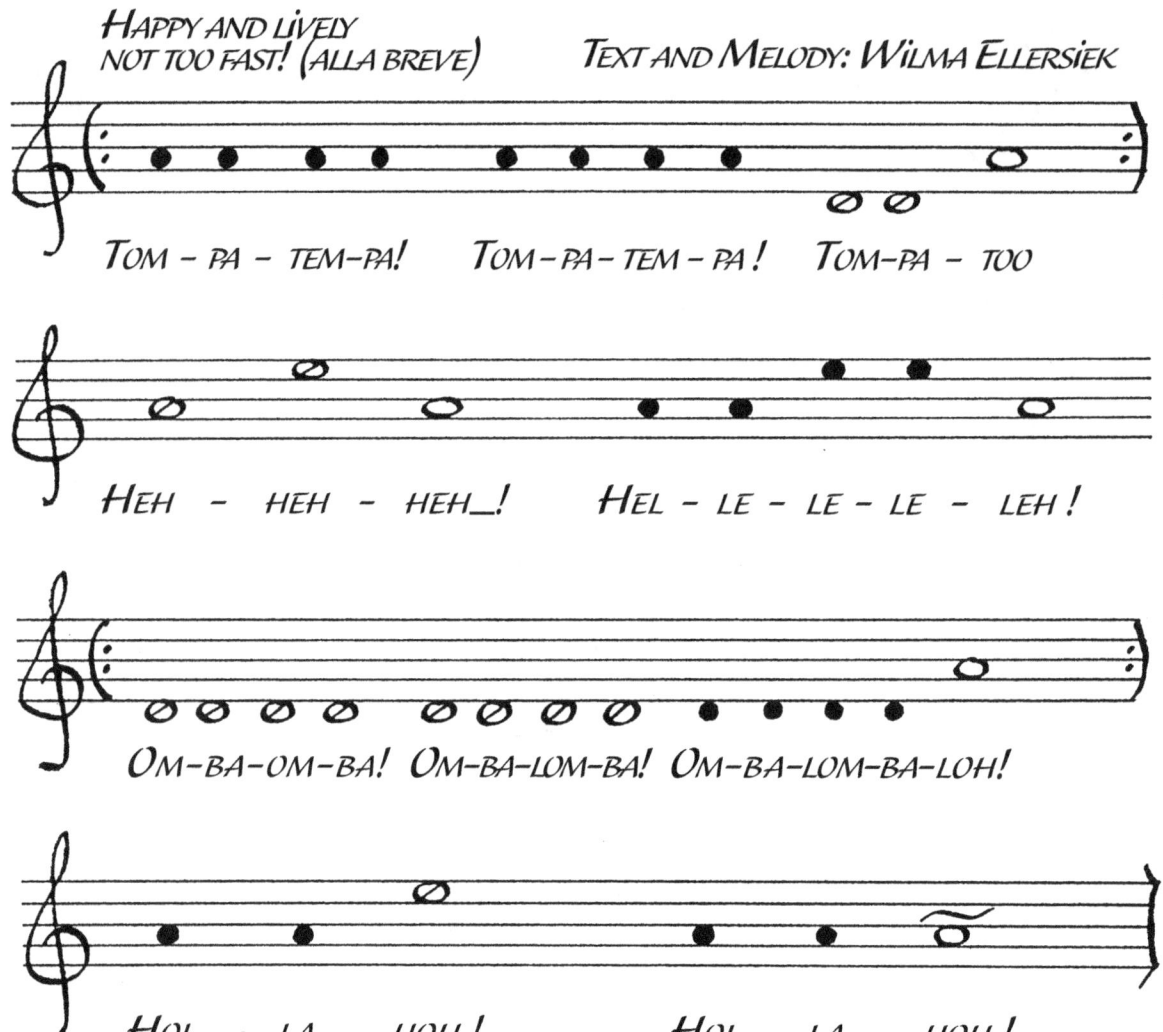

TEXT:	JINGLE STICK DIRECTIONS:
1 Tompa-tempa! 　　x　　x 　　　　　Tompa-tempa! 　　　　　　x　　x 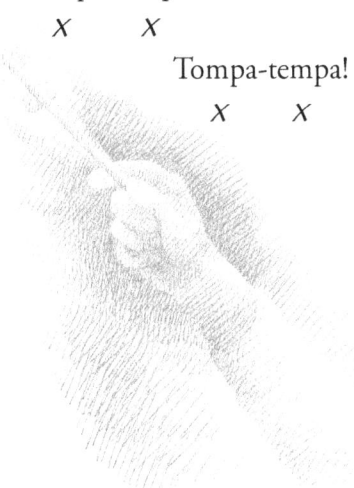	1 With your right hand hold the jingle stick to about head height. At "x," tip lightly in the air toward the front. Your whole arm should be relaxed as you do this.
2 Tom-pa-toooo! 　　x　x　x 	2 Rhythmically and gently tap on your right thigh with the jingle stick, three times. After the third time let the jingle stick hang down. Then raise the jingle stick upright while sounding a long "oo." It's like pulling it from a sticky dough.
3 Tompa-tempa! 　　　　　Tompa-tempa! 　 Tom-pa-toooo!	3 Repeat 1 and 2. Movements must be relaxed.
4 Heh-heh-heh! 　 ∧∧∧∧∧∧∧ 　　　　　Hel-le-le-le-leh! 　　　　　∧∧∧∧∧∧∧∧	4 Shake the jingle stick continuously to and fro, lightly and airily. Make sure of relaxed movements. Allow enough time to be ready from one movement to the next.
5 Om-ba-om-ba! 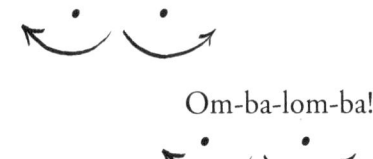 　　　　　Om-ba-lom-ba!	5 Stand the jingle stick upright on your left fist with a light bounce at " • ". The edge of your pinky is at the bottom of your fist. Thumbs and fingers are up and rolled in.

The Tompa-Tempa with the jingle stick is suitable for children five years or older. If there are younger children in the group, allow them to participate, but don't correct them. Generally speaking, do not correct the children but let them learn the game through repetition. For craft directions to make jingle sticks, see the appendix.

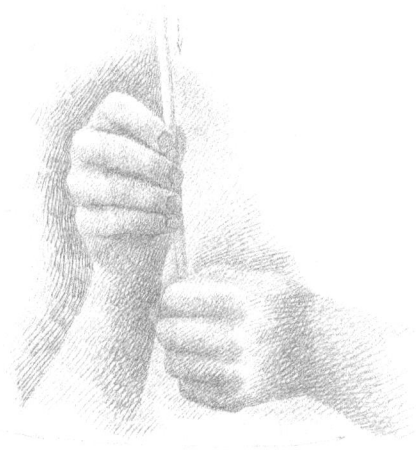

During this movement, slightly rock your left fist to and fro.

6 Om-ba-lom-ba-loh!

7 Omba-omba!
              Omba-lomba!
8 Omba-lomba-loh!
9 Hol-la-hoh! Hol-la-hoh!
10 *silent*

6 Continue as in 6. At "loh," slowly lift jingle stick from your left fist. Stretch the sound "ohoh" as you call in a nearly singing voice.
7 As in 6.
8 As in 6.
9 Lift the jingle stick high and shake it as in 4.
10 At the end, hold the jingle stick close to your ear, enclosing it with your left hand so that it cannot continue to sound. Listen until the small balls within each jingle stop moving and there is no more sound. Then lay the jingle stick in your lap, covering it with both of your hands.

Mock and Pock

*A*AH *–* Y*IP!*
*A*AH *–* Y*IP!*
*A*AH *–* Y*IP!*

*H*OOPPA *–* HOH*!*
*H*OOPPA *–* HOH*!*
*H*OOPPA *–* HOH*!*

*M*IMME *–* MOCK*!*
*M*IMME *–* MOCK*!*

*M*OCK *–* MOCK *–*
*A*ND POCK*!*

TEXT:

1   Aah –

2   yip!

GESTURES:

1   Sit on a stool or a chair. Speak a long, melodious, drawn-out "Aah," and, at the same time, lift your arms with stretched hands and fingers slanting upwards until your elbows are stretched. Make sure that your arms are not stretched too much. Your palms face toward your body.

2   Quickly place your hands in front of your chest and tap all your fingernails (except the thumbnails) together with a small, springy movement. The vowel "i" must coincide with the sound of your fingernails tapping at each other. For the "p" in "yip," make a small circle with your still bent fingers up

		and out, almost like bouncing back after a collision. Then lift your arms immediately for the next "Aah!" Repeat twice, varying the modulation of your voice.		
3	Hooppa –	3	At the "oo" and "a" of "hooppa," lightly pat your thighs with your flat hands.	**PRONUNCIATION:** "oo" short, as in "look."
4	hoh!	4	For "hoh," quickly raise your arms with hands and fingers stretched. This time your palms are turned to the children. Follow your hands with your eyes by slightly bending your head back. Repeat "hooppa – hoh!" twice, varying the modulation of your voice.	
5	Mimme –	5	Quickly return your hands to chest height. With your fingertips, at the "i" and "e" of "mimme," tap on your body at about the height of your collarbones.	
6	mock!	6	Push both of your arms forward, parallel, with your hands palms down and stretched into your fingertips, toward the children. Repeat 5 and 6 once more. Keep your arms and hands in this position.	
7	Mock – mock	7	At each "m" of "mock – mock," relax your elbows a little, but push forward again at "o." Pause after the second "mock," with your arms remaining in the stretched position. Look joyfully and expectantly at the children.	

8   And

9   pock!

8   With your arms in the stretched position, clap your flat hands at the word "and."

9   Quickly cross your lower arms and make your hands disappear under your arm pits. For children under four years old, let your hands disappear behind your back.

Part II: Trotting Pony

We Love all the Creatures

*We love all the creatures
As they crawl and creep,
And patter and spring,
And waddle and swim,
And leap and hop,
And slither and slink,
And flutter and fly,
And sleep and rest
In burrow and nest.*

*We love all the creatures
As they grumble and hum,
And chirp and feep,
And gabble and quack,
And chatter and crow
And bark and low,
And bleat and mew,
And call: "Hee-haw,"
And flute and sing:
Tiri – tirila,
Tiri – tirila!*

About Children and Animals

"To begin with, the Gods made the Heavens and the Earth, and the Earth was desolate and chaotic, and darkness covered the abyss; and the divine breath brooded over the waters. . . Then spake the divine Word: Let the waters be moved with wafting and living beasts and with fowl so that they may fly beneath the Firmament of the Heavens. And the Gods made great whales and all sorts of beast, living and weaving, moved by the waters, each according to its kind; and all sorts of bird, each according to its kind. And the Gods saw that all was good. . . And the divine Word spake: The Earth shall bring forth living beasts, each according to its kind: cattle, worms and beasts of the Earth, each according to its kind. And so it was. And the Gods made the beasts upon the Earth, each according to its kind, and the cattle according to their kind and all sorts of worm upon the Earth according to their kind. And the Gods saw that all was good."

(Genesis 1: verses 1, 2, 20-22, 24, 25)

Plants, beasts and human beings enliven the Earth. Animals live in almost all elements: some live under the earth's surface; a great variety live in the water; the air is filled with birds and insects. The beasts are fellow-creatures endowed with soul. A number of them have been tamed and put into human service. Most, however, live in our surroundings, hardly noticed by modern human beings. Each one, however, has its purpose and its right to existence given through its place in the mutual play of natural events.

To children, animals are friends. Most children trustingly approach even large animals, feeling the need for contact with these beings. Often, the first contact is made through touch: the child's hand discovers if an animal is warm and furry, or if it is cold, slippery or even may have sharp quills or spines. A second form of contact is through quietly, wonderingly watching the animals. At first, without expressing sympathy or antipathy toward what they see, the children take in what is essential about the animal. They are not put off or disgusted by spiders, worms, snails; to the contrary, many a small animal offers up its life for the sake of children's handling, curiosity, and natural searching drive.

Children between the ages of two and six especially like to pretend to be animals in their play. Depending on the situation, they become mighty beasts exuding power, or again a soft cuddly bunny or kitten. To bring a strong urge for movement into action, one might become a horse, a monkey or even a frog. Such changes take absolute form in the children. They don't just act "like" a lion or a donkey, but really "are" the lion or donkey. Thanks to the strong power of the children's imaginations, they see themselves perfectly in their animal-role, and react with outrage when adults don't see the "lion" or the "donkey." To slip into the role of an animal makes possible for children the assumption of characteristics and attributes that they would wish for themselves. Children especially, like to turn themselves into lions, tigers or bears, in which roles they are no longer small, but much more powerful than any adult.

In our cities, children seldom get to know animals in their natural surroundings. Today's children see pictures of animals in books or movies more often than in nature, or else they have cloth or plastic toy animals. Very often, however, such toy animals are caricatured to such an extent that even an adult can hardly tell a rabbit from a dog. Also, in so-called children's cartoon films, ever and again grotesque figures portray a hybrid of animal and human. Are these figures humanized beasts, or are they people degenerated into animals?

What is certain is that such examples damage the children's souls, since small children aren't yet able to distinguish between what is genuine and what is a caricature. For a pre-school child, everything is genuine, and even an exaggerated drawing will be taken as truth.

There are of course also pictures and movies that portray animals realistically. Still, even here the children only get a weak two-dimensional substitute for the actual experience of living animals in their natural habitat. In toy animals, pictures, etc., a true-to-nature copy of outer appearance is not important, but only that some essential attribute of the particular animal is given fitting expression.

Apart from pictures or toy animals, there is still another way to convey to children something "alive" about the character of certain animals: the hand-gesture game. If an adult makes the effort to come as close as possible by means of gesture and movement to what is typical of a particular animal, the child will experience that animal as living and true. As mentioned above, the power of imagination in the first five or six years of life are so intensely present that before the inner eye of the child the hand-gesture of the adult, made with faithful intention, becomes a "real" animal. Once done, a practiced and successfully carried out hand-gesture game can be repeated as often as is wished. That fulfills very well the child's needs; for a child, something done once only is as good as not done at all. Repetition of hand-gesture games inspires children to do it too. Finally, the children learn and experience, through imitation, something characteristic about the animal portrayed through play.

One special point still needs to be emphasized about the games of Wilma Ellersiek: the animals are shown through play, acting in their natural way. They never begin to speak; never move in ways they would not be able to move; never are they portrayed as quasi-human. Wilma Ellersiek limits speech only to actions, renouncing any description or emotional language, just as the children themselves see it—as true.

Ingrid Weidenfeld

Living Water and Bread of Life
A Call to Deeds

Whoever the threshold has never crossed
Knows not what children through time have lost
At the world's hands, which has forgot to wonder,
Which of each thing only the name can ponder,
And of its primal gesture nothing knows
By which himself the Creator-Spirit shows.

She cannot recognize the children's need,
Those to whom stones are given in place of bread,
Whose gentle souls' deep thirst meets but dry ground,
Whose spirit-being suffers many a wound.

Because of this, for humans I appeal,
Who in themselves the secret can reveal!
So let these people hear my call:
"Work tirelessly, rest not at all.
Work and strive for ears and eyes and mind,
Worthy the Creator-Spirit to find.
The power of Love your footsteps sure will guide,
Truth to find, and pass it far and wide:

Living Water and Life's Bread!

Bring this to the children, assuage their need,
Till all children by this Deed are blest."

Wilma Ellersiek

Translation by Lyn Willwerth
Easter Monday, 1994

The Earthworm

Rhythmic-Musical Game for the Pointer

The earthworm likes to writhe and squirm.
He curls into a ring, the worm.
Makes himself long – and short – and long.
Bores a hole in the ground:
Bores – bo-o-ores – bo-o-o-o-ores.
Slips into his hole small
With head, tail and all.

TEXT:	HAND GESTURES:
1 *In Preparation: silent movement*	1 With your right hand form a loose fist; your thumb lies on top of your other fingers. Place your fist, fingers down, on your right thigh, close to your upper body.
2 The earthworm 	2 Stick out your right pointer, making sure that the fingertip always touches your thigh. As you do this, turn your fist slightly unto the edge of your pinky, so that your pointer touches your thigh with the edge. Do this movement very slowly and smoothly.
3 likes to writhe and squirm.	3 At "likes," slowly move your pointer forward toward your knee. At "writhe," continue moving your fist forward, but a little to the left, led by your fingertip. At "and," the worm moves to the right, at "squirm," again to the left. Your pointer is held still during this flowing movement.

4 He curls into a ring,
   the worm.

4 At "he," move again to the right, stop the forward movement and at "curls," curl your pointer as far as possible.

5 Makes himself long –

5 Stretch your pointer as in 2, at the same time resuming the forward movement of your fist.

6 and short – and long.

6 At "short," continue moving forward very slowly, while curling your pointer as in 4. At "long," stretch it again. Speak the word "long" very slowly and, according to your speech, stretch your pointer far out.

7 *Silent movement*

7 Now put your left hand on your right thigh, fingers close together, and fingertips touching your knee. Fold your thumb underneath, for your hand to form an arch: Your left hand forms a hill.

8 Bores a hole in the ground:

8 The earthworm creeps to the little hill. At the place where your thumb is curled underneath your hand, the worm bores into the earth once, to and fro, without moving forward. Pause.

9 Bores – bo-o-ores –
   bo-o-o-o-ores.

9 Now the worm moves forward again along your left thumb as you slowly speak the second "bo-o-ores". At the same time, the worm wiggles to the right, the left, and again the right, as shown

by the arrows. Pause. Repeat the movements for the third "bo-o-o-ores" as before, but with an additional turn. Pause.

10 Slips into his hole small 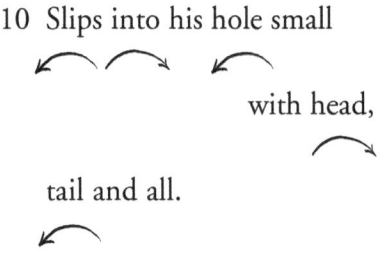 with head, tail and all.

10 In the suggested rhythm the worm continues to bore until the right pointer has completely disappeared in the hill. Hold the last movement for a little while.

The Snail

Rhythmic-Musical Hand Gesture Game

The snail, she sits inside her shell,
Looks out and stretches her feelers well,
And starts to crawl along.
Crawls – crawls – crawls –
So slowly she gets on.
Crawls – crawls – crawls – and stops.
Is tired, draws her feelers in,
And rests now in her shell within.

TEXT:	HAND GESTURES:
1 *Silent movement*	1 Make a loose fist with your right hand. Your thumb lies on your fingers. Your fist lies on a surface, for example: on your thigh, a table, the floor etc.
2 The snail, she sits inside her shell,	2 Look at your "snail" and speak thoughtfully.
3 Looks out and stretches her feelers well,	3 Still looking at your snail, very slowly stick out your pointer and then your pinky as "feelers."
4 And starts to crawl along.	4 Slowly the snail starts to move.
5 Crawls – crawls – crawls –	5 Keep slowly but continuously moving your snail forward. Speak in a very stretched way, always at the same pitch. Your fist may only barely touch the "ground" so that the

Depending on age and motor development, the children will imitate the snail's feelers with thumb and pointer or pointer and middle finger. Don't correct them. Eventually they will discover by themselves that your hand looks different. They need sufficient time to become more precise in their imitation.

6   So slowly she gets on.

7   Crawls – crawls – crawls –

8   and stops.

9   Is tired,

10 draws her feelers in,

11 And rests now in
    her shell within.

movement stays flexible. Make small breaks in-between words, but do not stop the forward movement. After the third "crawls," the snail stops.

6   Look at the snail while slowly speaking the text. At the same time, move the "feelers" a little. Thereafter, the snail continues on her journey, moving forward very slowly.

7   Continue crawling as in 5. The snail may also slightly change direction by a movement from the wrist of your "snail hand."

8   Stop the movement and look at your snail.

9   At: "tired," nod your head once. Take a brief pause, then move the feelers a little.

10 Slowly roll back your pointer and pinky, returning to the position in 1.

11 Look at your fist (snail) lying quietly on your thigh. Leave yourself plenty of time before dissolving this gesture.

Hustle Hoosh!
Hand Gesture Game

From her house peeps the mouse: feep – feep!
Hustles: hoosh – hoosh – hoosh – hoosh!
Finds a little nut:
P p p p p p p p! Nibbles the mouse.
P p p p p p p p! Nibble – nibble – nouse.
Feep! Feep!
Hustles: hoosh – hoosh – hoosh – hoosh!
Finds a little root:
T t t t t t t t! Gnaws the mouse.
T t t t t t t t! Nubba – nubba – nouse.
In the forest it goes: Crack!
hoosh – hoosh: she runs back! Feep!

TEXT:		HAND GESTURES:	
1	From her house	1	Lay your rounded left hand on your right thigh, close to your body, palm down. With your right hand, put your pointer and middle finger on top of your thumb, your fingertips extend slightly over your thumb tip, forming the "mouse's nose." Hide the little nose under your rounded left hand.
2	peeps the mouse:	2	At "peeps," the little nose suddenly appears from under the "mouse hole," the rounded left hand.
3	feep – feep! *left right*	3	The little mouse looks left and right at: "feep – feep."

4 Hustles: hoosh – hoosh –
　↑　　↗　　↖
　　　　hoosh – hoosh!
　　　　　　↗　　↖

4 At "hustle," the little mouse leaves its hole and runs quickly along a short stretch of your thigh toward your knee. Then he stops suddenly. At each "hustle" or "hoosh," again move him quickly forward, but in changing directions, so that the mouse runs in zigzags towards your knee. At your knee, stop the movement again. While the mouse hustles, dissolve unnoticed the mouse hole gesture of your left hand.

5 Finds a little nut:

5 At the word "finds," lightly press the little nose down into the ground (your right knee.)

6 P p p p p p p p!
　　　nibbles the mouse.
　P p p p p p p p!
　　　Nibble – nibble – nouse.

6 With your pointer and middle finger tap with quick, tiny, rhythmic movements on the tip of your thumb. This movement shows the nibbling of the mouse. For the "ppppppp" pucker your lips as if giving a kiss, opening and closing your lips very fast while sucking in the air a little. This creates a nibbling noise. Movements of the "mouse" should be coordinated with the sounds. Take a brief break at the end of each text line.

7 Feep! Feep!
　↖　↗

7 The little mouse looks left and right, and each time he does he calls "feep!"

8   Hustles: hoosh – hoosh –
    ↓   ↘   ↗
            hoosh – hoosh!
                ↘   ↗

8   Suddenly the little mouse hustles back to the left, running along the inside of your thigh, but still close to your knee. (Don't turn your "mouse hand," the little nose is always pointed to the children.) Then stop suddenly. Run him zigzag along your thigh toward your body. Stop suddenly.

9   Finds a little root:
    V   *V*   *V*

9   Bend your pointer and middle fingers so that they can scratch your thigh or other surface. Also bend your thumb. This gesture suggests the "teeth of the little mouse." Scratch the surface at each "*V*."

10 T t t t t t t t!
          gnaws the mouse.

    T t t t t t t!
        Nubba – nubba – nouse.

10 Rhythmically gnaw an imaginary root with your "mouse teeth." In other words, the finger nails scratch on the support surface. To make a gnawing sound, press your tongue against the roof of your mouth directly behind the upper teeth. Suck in the air a little, and very quickly move your tongue back and forth from the roof of your mouth. Pause at the end of each line.

11 In the forest it goes:

11 Speak the text: "in the forest it goes" quickly, softly, well articulated, and at the same pitch.

12 Crack!
    •

12 Suddenly call out short and high: "Crack!" tapping your thigh quickly with your left pointer. This

	"crack" is an acorn which has fallen down.
13 Hoosh – hoosh: she runs back!	13 The little mouse disappears behind your back in zigzag. Take a brief pause.
14 Feep!	14 The mouse nose appears once more at "feep." It looks boldly around the corner, then disappears again behind your back.

The Cat

Rhythmic-Musical Hand Gesture Game

Who sneaks along with silent tread?
It is the cat! Mew.
In the warm sun she keeps.
Aye-aye – Purrs: prr-prr-prr.
Aye-aye – prr-prr.
Aye – prr –
And sleeps.

TEXT:

1 *silent:* — — — —
           P   M   P   M
   Who sneaks along with
           P   M
           silent tread?
           P   M
   silent: — — — —
           P   M   P   M

HAND GESTURES:

1 Your right hand is the cat. For the sneaking motion of a cat, form a fist with your right hand, stretch out your slightly bent pointer and middle finger, and put your thumb on the curled ring finger. The cat sneaks from the right hip very slowly and smoothly across your right thigh. For the sneaking, touch your thigh very carefully with the fingertips of your pointer and middle finger in turn. For each step of the cat, stretch out the corresponding finger far ahead, as if the cat gropes along the floor. The cat walks her first four steps silently. Continue, fitting the words to the movement, followed by four more steps silently. Now the cat has reached your knee.

2 It is the cat!

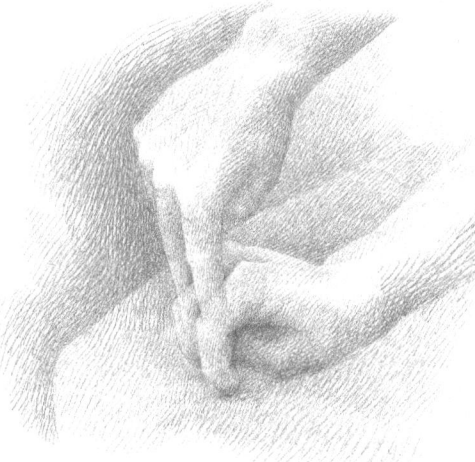

2 The cat stops. At "it is the," she humps her back. Raise your right wrist as high as possible without the "paws" leaving your thigh. The movement of pulling up your wrist continues all the way up to your shoulder. (Try to visualize how, when a cat makes a hump, the tension in the muscles travels through its whole body.) At the word "cat," form your right hand into a loose fist again lying on your thigh.

3 Mew.

3 With your wrist resting firmly on your thigh, lift and then replace your right fist while saying: "Mew." Create a musical tone for "mew," not a naturalistic one.

4 In the warm sun she keeps.

4 Lovingly gaze at the cat. Speak the text so that one can feel the warm sunshine!

5 Aye-aye –

5 At each "aye," stroke lovingly with your left hand across fist and lower arm up to your elbow. Speak "aye-aye" in a sing-song tone. Then bend your right ear in the direction of the cat, and listen.

6 Purrs: prr-prr-prr.

6 Speak the "prr" three times at the same tone height. Roll your "r" with your tongue if possible. Purse your lips while rolling your "r." That gives the purring a lovely, dark sound.

7 Aye-aye – prr-prr.
   Aye - prr –
8 And sleeps.

7 As in 5 and 6. After the last "prr," listen a little longer.
8 Look at the cat. Now, very slowly, turn your right fist on the edge of your pinky and bend your wrist strongly to the left, the cat curls up to sleep. Draw out the words accompanying this movement. At the last word your fist lies immobile on your thigh. Look silently but happily at the children, nodding your head once.

Flutter Flutter

Flutter – flutter, flee – flah – flutter,
Flutter – flutter – butterfly,
Flutter-by! Flutter-by!

She sits down upon my knee!
Out and in, out and in she flaps her wing,
See, but see! See, but see!

Flutter – flutter, flee – flah – flutter,
Flutter – flutter – butterfly,
Flutter-by! Flutter-by!

She sits down upon my nose!
Out and in, out and in she flaps her wing,
Tickletoes! Tickletoes!

Flutter – flutter, flee – flah – flutter,
Flutter – flutter – butterfly,
Flutter-by! Flutter-by!

Finds a flower, my flutter guest.
Out and in, out and in she flaps her wing,
In the sunshine, flutter-thing,
Cozy, warm, she takes a rest.

TEXT:	HAND GESTURES:
1 Flut-ter – flut-ter, flee – flah – flut-ter, Flut-ter – flut-ter – but-ter-fly – , 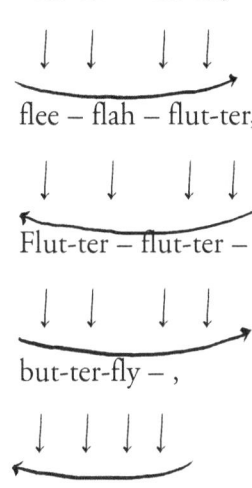	1 Your right hand is the "butterfly." Fingers and thumb are tightly pressed against each other and stretched. They are the "wing" of the butterfly. For flying, lift up your right hand, palm down. In the speech rhythm, move your fingers very quickly up and down. The movement originates at the base of your fingers. Your fingers remain stretched and your wrist immobile. Flutter as the arrows show, that is, as the flight direction changes in the middle of the line.
2 Flutter-by! Flutter-by! 	2 The butterfly flies with many flutter movements, as shown in the directional arrows. Speak very melodiously and drawn out—almost singing.
3 *Silent movement* 	3 With many small flutter movements, fly from the right side to your right knee.
4 She sits down upon my knee! 	4 At: "she sits," turn the fluttering butterfly with your palm up (while continuing fluttering) and at "down," set your hand on your thigh with the middle finger a handbreadth from your knee. Now stretch the wing up and hold it still. The outside of your fingers looks toward the children. Look lovingly at the butterfly.

This game was created during a course with Japanese nursery school teachers and I therefore dedicate it especially to the Japanese children. But all other children in the world may enjoy this game.

5 Out and in, out and in
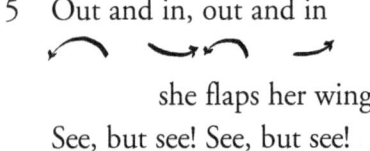
    she flaps her wing,
   See, but see! See, but see!

6 Flutter – flutter,
   ↓ ↓ ↓ ↓
   flee – flah – flutter,
   ↓ ↓ ↓ ↓
   Flutter – flutter –
   ↓ ↓ ↓ ↓
   butterfly-
   ↓ ↓ ↓ ↓

7 Flutter-by! Flutter-by!

8 *Silent movement*

9 She sits down upon
                    my nose!

10 Out and in, out and in
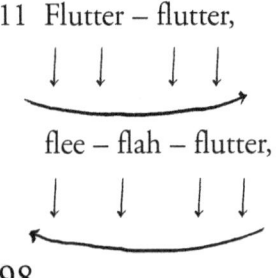
    she flaps her wing,
   Tickletoes! Tickletoes!

11 Flutter – flutter,
   ↓ ↓ ↓ ↓
   flee – flah – flutter,
   ↓ ↓ ↓ ↓

5 Now move your stretched fingers, wing, down until it touches your knee, then lift them up again to the previous position. Do this movement slowly and quietly in the given rhythm, it is almost like rocking to a lullaby.

6 As in 1.

7 As in 2.

8 With many small flutter movements fly in an arc to your nose.

9 At: "She sits," turn your fluttering butterfly and set it on the bridge of your nose, palm to the children. At "down," hold your hand still.

10 Flap with the stretched, tightly closed fingers of your wing until the backs of your fingers touch your cheek, then return to the original position. Continue as in 5.

11 As in 1.

Flutter – flutter –

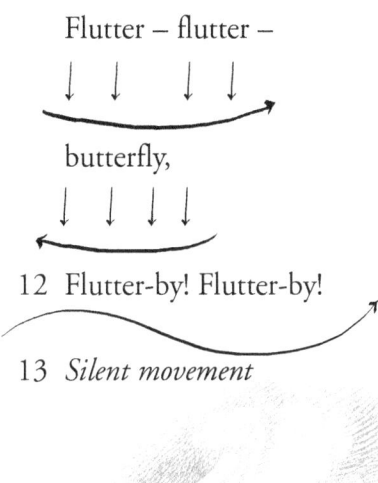

butterfly,

12 Flutter-by! Flutter-by!   12 As in 2.

13 *Silent movement*   13 As in 3. The left hand forms a flower.

14 Finds a flower,   14 As in 4.
      my flutter guest.

15 Out and in, out and in   15 As in 5. However, at the end the wing is opened once more and remains in this position.

      she flaps her wing,

16 In the sunshine,   16 The butterfly remains sitting on the "flower" with open wing. It is warmed by the sun.
      flutter-thing,

17 cozy, warm, she takes a rest.   17 Hold wing upright, then turn until your fingertips lie on the ball of your thumb. End the game in a light, soft voice.
This game may be ended with a lullaby, sung or played. While singing, gently swing the blossom with the butterfly to and fro.

Loo-loo-loo

Rocking   *Text and Melody: Wilma Ellersiek*

Loo-loo-loo! Now he rests, the flut-ter-thing.
Loo-loo-loo! Clos-es tight his tir-ed wing.

Now he rests, the flut-ter-thing. Loo-loo-loo!
Clos-es tight his tir-ed wing. Loo-loo-loo!

Notation: ⊘ ≈ one calm, swinging pulsation (Basic unit) / •• ≈ ⊘ / o ≈ ⊘⊘ / ~ ≈ sustain longer / (: :) ≈ repeat / ⌣ ≈ phrase

    This game can also be played as a touch game. Mother, father or other caregiver lets the butterfly fly to the child's knee, nose or flower (right hand) and flaps her wing out and in. You can also play the opposite way: the child lets his or her butterfly fly to the game partner. Of course, the butterfly can fly to other body parts and flap her wing open and shut there. You can then use the following rhyme: "Out and in, out and in she flaps her wing, butterfly, the flutter-thing." The butterfly can also fly to other targets. Try to include the children's ideas, even if they are a little strange to you.

The Birdie
Rhythmic-Musical Hand Gesture Game

Birdie in his nest at night
Sleeps so tight.

When the morning breaks,
He awakes.

Twitters softly:
Tiwitt-tiwitt – titt-titt.
Tiwitt-tiwitt – titt-titt.

Off the little birdie flies,
Wings – wings – wings –
Again sits down and sings:
Cheep – cheep – cheer,
You're my dear, you're my dear!
On the little birdie flies,
Wings – wings – wings –
Finds some little seeds to peck!

Peck-peck-peck-peck-peck-peck-pay!
He pecks all the seeds away.
On the little birdie flies,
Wings – wings – wings –
Finds a water-well.
Dips! – Sips! – Tilts his head with the drop.
It rolls: glook-glook-glook-glook into his crop.
Dips! – Sips! – Glook-glook-glook-glook.
Dips! – Sips! – Glook-glook-glook-glook.
On the little birdie flies,
Wings – wings – wings –
Finds a branch to sit,
And rests a bit.
For all good things, thanks he sings.

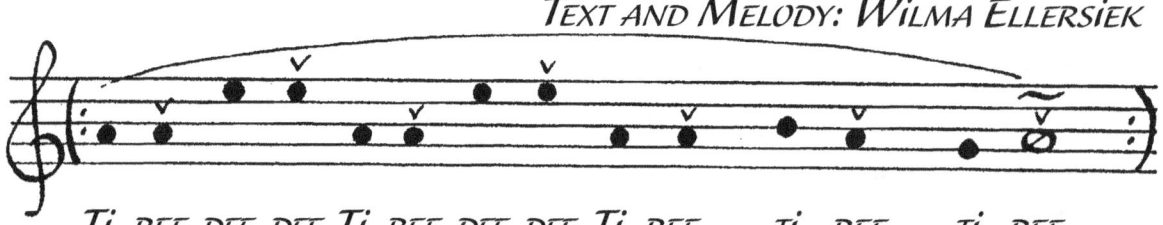

Ti-ree-dee-dee, Ti-ree-dee-dee, Ti-ree – ti-ree – ti-ree.

Notation: ● ≈ one pulsation in a middle temp /⊘ ≈ ●●/
∨ ≈ stress note while singing / ~ ≈ sustain longer / (: :) ≈
repeat / ⌒ ≈ phrase

On the little birdie flies,
Wings – wings – wings –
Flies back home into his nest,
And keeps rest. And keeps rest.
Under his wing he puts his head,
Sleeps cozily in his wee bed.
Let us ask the dear wind mild:
"Rock our little birdie child."

Blow Wind, Blow So Mild

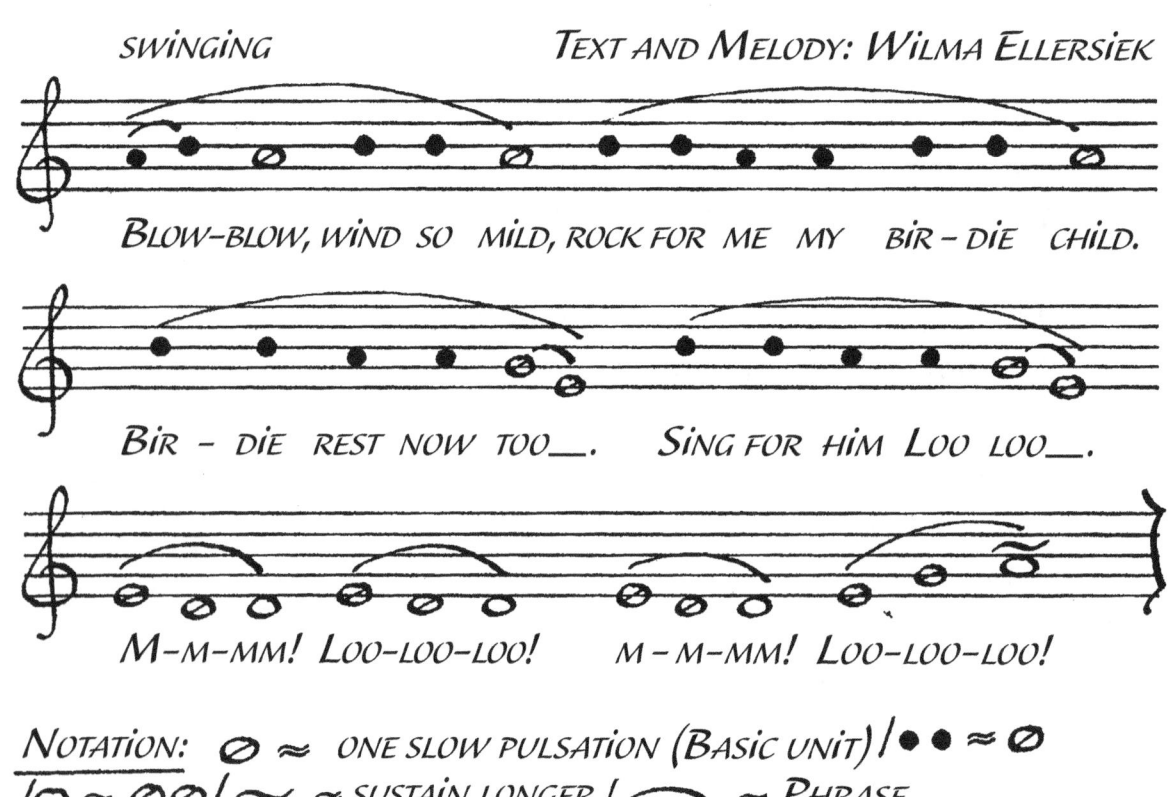

Notation: ⊘ ≈ one slow pulsation (basic unit) / ●● ≈ ⊘
/⊘ ≈ ⊘⊘/ ~ ≈ sustain longer / ⌒ ≈ phrase

TEXT:	GESTURES:
1 Birdie	1 Form a "beak" with the pointer and thumb of your right hand (your other fingers are rolled in.) Your left hand forms a bowl, the "nest."
2 in his nest at night	2 Set the little birdie into the nest.

3 Sleeps so tight.	3 Roll your right pointer and thumb inward, as if the birdie sticks his beak under his wing.
4 When the morning breaks	4 Lightly lift up the nest with the sleeping birdie.
5 He awakes.	5 Again form the beak with pointer and thumb looking out over the rim of the nest, as in 2.
6 Twitters softly: Tiwitt-tiwitt – titt-titt. < < < < Tiwitt-tiwitt – titt-titt. < < < <	6 At each "<" open and close the beak with a very small movement. Speak rhythmically. Look at the birdie as it twitters, then listen after it, smiling at the children. Then again look at the birdie.
7 Off the little birdie flies, Wings – wings – wings –	7 Dissolve the nest gesture. Your right hand changes into a flying bird. Stretch all fingers while holding them tightly together, including your thumb. The flight movement originates in your

8 Again sits down and sings:

9 Cheep – cheep – cheer.
      <   <   **<**
You're my dear,
      <   <   **<**
            you're my dear!
              <   <   **<**

10 On the little birdie flies,
~~~~~~~~~~
Wings – wings – wings –
~~~~~~~~~~

11 Finds some little seeds
                  to peck!

12 Peck-peck-peck-peck-peck-
   o   o   o   o   o
              peck-pay
               o   o
He pecks all the seeds away
 o   o   o   o   o
Peck-peck-peck-peck-
  o   o   o   o
              peck-peck-pay
               o   o   o
He pecks all the seeds away
 o   o   o   o   o

13 On the little birdie flies,
~~~~~~~~~~
Wings – wings – wings –
~~~~~~~~~~

---

right wrist and continues smoothly through all of your fingers into your fingertips. The movement is light and relaxed and moves up and down rhythmically with your speech. The birdie flies in an arc to the right, then returns to his original position with another arc.

8 Your right hand forms the beak again and sits down with the wrist close to your knee. The birdie sits there for a short while.

9 The beak points toward the children and opens and shuts in the given speech rhythm. <, marks a small beak opening; **<**, a larger opening.

10 As in 7.

11 As in 8, but sit in the middle of your right thigh.

12 With the tip of the beak, peck rhythmically for imaginary seeds all around on your thigh. For this pecking movement lift your wrist slightly from your thigh.

13 As in 7.

14 Finds a water-well.

15 Dips! – Sips!
        <<<

16 Tilts his head with the drop.

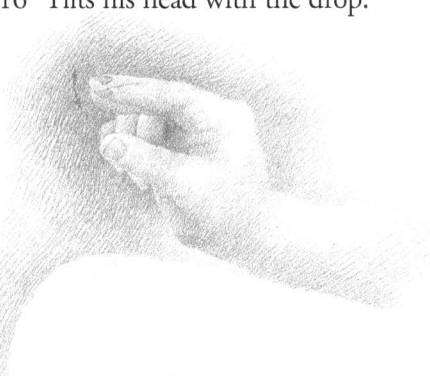

17 It rolls: glook-glook-glook-
      <   <   <
    glook into his crop.
    < << < <

18 Dips! – Sips!
19 Glook-glook-glook-glook.
    <   <   <   <

20 Dips! – Sips! –
    Glook-glook-glook-glook.
    <   <   <   <

21 On the little birdie flies,
    Wings – wings – wings –
22 Finds a branch to sit,

14 As in 8, but sit close to your upper body.

15 At the word: "dips," tip with the "beak" on your thigh as if you were dipping it into water. Again your wrist lifts up slightly but returns back immediately to its former position. At "sips," birdie sits as in 14 and his beak opens and shuts fast in a very small movement: open-shut-open.

16 Turn your right hand back at the wrist with the beak slightly open.

17 In this position rhythmically move the "beak" very fast, never completely shutting it. Speak the text fast, starting the tone high and moving it down.

18 Repeat 15.
19 Swallow the "drop" in small, fast movements of the beak as described in 17.
20 As in 18 and 19.

21 As in 7.

22 While the birdie is still flying, make a fist with your left hand and stick out your pointer. Hold your fist

with the back of your hand toward the children. With your right hand form a beak again and let the birdie sit down on the branch – your left pointer.

23 And rests a bit.

23 The birdie sits quietly as you look at him fondly.

24 For all good things
thanks he sings.

24 Look at the children and nod at "good things" and "sings."

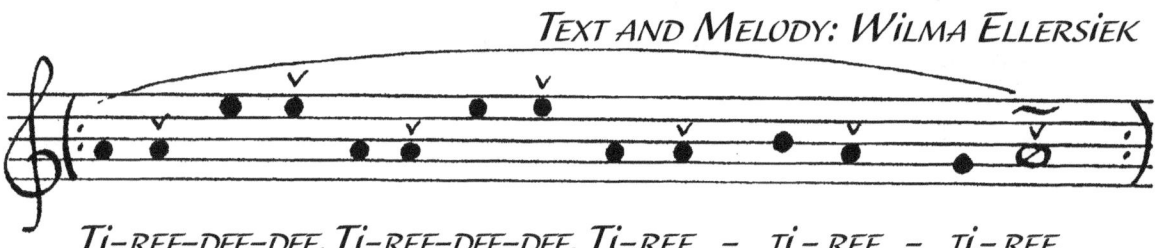

TEXT AND MELODY: WILMA ELLERSIEK

Ti-ree-dee-dee, Ti-ree-dee-dee, Ti-ree – ti-ree – ti-ree.

NOTATION: ● ≈ ONE PULSATION IN A MIDDLE TEMP |⌀ ≈ ●●|
ᵛ ≈ STRESS NOTE WHILE SINGING / ~ ≈ SUSTAIN LONGER / (: :) ≈
REPEAT / ⌒ ≈ PHRASE

25 On the little birdie flies,
Wings – wings – wings –

25 As in 7.

26 Flies back home into
his nest,

26 While the birdie is still flying, form a nest with your left hand as in 1. At the word "nest," quickly change the flying birdie into the beak gesture and set it into the nest.

27 And keeps rest.
And keeps rest.

27 The birdie sits comfortably in his nest, only his beak looks over the nest rim. At "rest," nod your head.

28 Under his wing he puts
his head,
Sleeps cozily in his
wee bed.

28 As in 3.

29 Let us ask the dear
          wind mild:
    "Rock our little
              birdie child."

29 Speak to the children while rocking the sleeping birdie gently to and fro. Then start the song, continuing the rocking motion.

Blow Wind, Blow So Mild

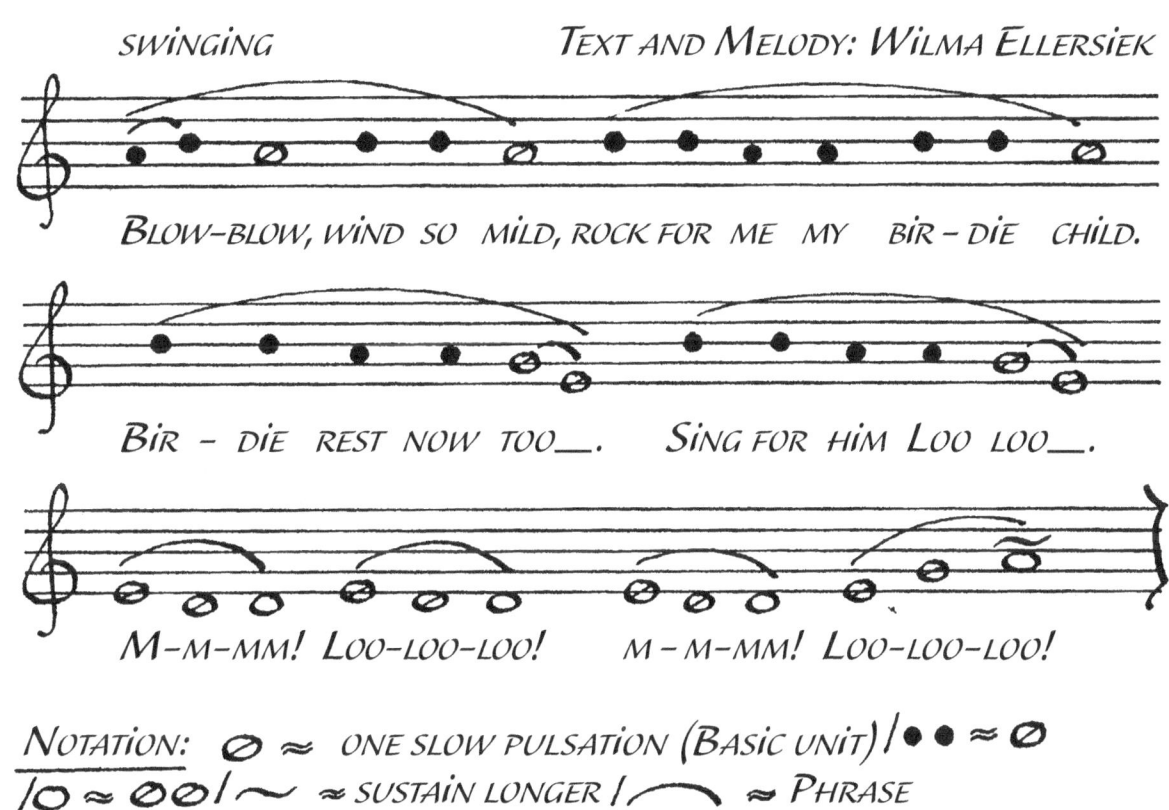

When the song is ended, listen after it for a bit and then slowly dissolve the gesture. Rest your hands on your thighs.

This hand gesture game may be shortened depending on the age of the children or the general play situation. For example, one can play points 1 through 7, skip a large portion, and continue at 26 until the end.

Another possibility: Points 1-7, then continue with 11, 12, and 13, then 26 to the end. The refrain: "on the little birdie flies, wings-wings-wings…" allows the possibility to arrange the other parts at will.

It is suitable to continue with the Woodpecker Song or the many bird calls in the Bird Concert. These games may be found in the book *Hand Gesture Games for Spring and Summer* by Wilma Ellersiek.

The Birdie Movement Game

Rhythmic-Musical Movement Game

In The Birdie Movement Game, the hand gestures of the previous game are transformed into spatial movements or are retained as hand gestures. The introductory positions can be assumed in various ways:

1. All the children sit in a circle on stools or on their heels on the floor, faces hidden in their hands or bent low. (This position is especially suitable for the youngest children or for mixed groups with younger and older children; it is most suitable if play space is limited.)
2. Children sit at random on the floor on their heels.
3. Use colored cotton ropes to make circular nests for the children to sit in.
4. The children sit, and you lay the ropes around them.
5. The children lay down their own ropes, and build their own nests.
6. You build the nests, then call each birdie, by name, into his or her nest. Make a nest for yourself, too.

Use the introductory positions that best fit your space, the children's ages, your group size and group character. Try to avoid the children colliding with each other as they fly. The simplest way is to fly in a circle (more or less.) It is most desirable to let the children fly freely in the room if enough space is available. Since you set the example in speech and movement, it is even more important to speak rhythmically and musically, as it provides impulse and motion.

Your voice should sound like an instrument, so that your speech can be experienced as activation of movement, sound and gestures. What should motivate the children is not meaning and image of speech, but that sound, syllable, and word be taken in as a sense experience. The formative forces of your speech should penetrate the children's whole organism.

Quiet-as-a-Mouse - Hoppa-Hop
Rhythmic-Musical Movement Game

In the grass, the bunny there,
Nose in the air, sniff, sniff,
Wagging with his tail, ears held stiff,
Starts to dance:

Hopsa-hopsa! Hopsassa! Hopsassa! Hopsassa!
Hopsa-hopsa! Trallala! Trallala! Trallala!
Hopsa-hopsa! Hopsassa! Hopsassa! Hopsassa!
Hopsa-hopsa! Trallala! Trallala! Trallala!

Pricks up his ears – listens – runs a pace –
Hop-hop, to his hiding-place! Sits quite still.
With his big, long ears can hear
That the fox is coming near.
Sits quiet as a mouse.
Quiet-as-a-mouse.

Listens – looks – fox went away.
Bunny is alone – hurray!

Sits again in the grass,
Nose in the air, sniff, sniff,
Wagging his tail, ears held stiff,
Starts to dance.

Hopsa-hopsa! Hopsassa! Hopsassa! Hopsassa!
Hopsa-hopsa! Trallala! Trallala! Trallala!
Hopsa-hopsa! Hopsassa! Hopsassa! Hopsassa!
Hopsa-hopsa! Trallala! Trallala! Trallala!

Ending:
Snuggles into a grassy nest,
In the shining sun must rest.
Comes a gentle wind so mild,
Sings softly for my bunny child.

Wind-soo-soo

Quietly floating and swinging — Text and Melody: Wilma Ellersiek

Sings the wind mild for the bun-ny child

Soo-soo-soo! Soo-soo-soo! Soo_, Soo_, Soo_ Soo_!!
Soo-soo-soo! Soo-soo-soo! Soo_, Soo_, Soo_ Soo_!

NOTATION: ● ≈ ONE PULSATION (BASIC UNIT) | ⊘ ≈ ● ● |
○ ≈ ● ● ● ● / (: :) ≈ REPEAT | ⊘ ⊘ ≈ SUSTAIN | ~ ≈ SUSTAIN LONGER
| ⁓⁓⁓ ≈ DIE OUT, AT THE SAME TIME SLOWER AND SOFTER
| ⌢ ≈ PHRASE

TEXT:

1 In the grass,
     the bunny there,

2 Nose in the air, sniff, sniff

MOVEMENTS:

1 To start the game, stand with slightly bent knees, with your hands against your chest as "paws." You could also crouch with your hands against your chest.

2 In the same position, cup your hands around your mouth, with your right fingertips on top of the fingernails of your left hand. Your thumbs rest with their nails on your upper lip. Your pointers lie on the bridge of your nose. Pulse lightly with

Quiet-as-a-Mouse can be extended by further play events. Aside from the fox, a dog or a hunter may come, or all three. The play as such will remain the same; only the name of the feared arrival needs to be changed. Play the ending only when no one else arrives.

The movement game can be played within a wide circle of stools or chairs. Especially for younger children, the circle of stools provides order and security. Therefore, in the beginning of the game, within a circle of stools, stand before your own stool and start with the "bunny posture" as described in 1.

3 Wagging with his tail, –

↑ ↓ ↑ ↓ ↑ ↓

4 ears held stiff,

5 Starts to dance:

6 Hopsa-hopsa!

7 Hopsassa! Hopsassa!
                        Hopsassa!

8 Hopsa-hopsa!
9 Trallala! Trallala! Trallala!
    r / r / r /

your fingers on your nose: the bunny sniffs.

3 Standing in position as in 1, put your hands behind your back. All fingers are rolled in and your thumbs touch. Rhythmically waggle your "tail."

4 Now put your hands against your head, with your fingers stretched and together and your palms forward, as "ears." (Don't correct young children if they hold the ears further down their heads.)

5 Lift arms and hands so that your ellbows are about head height. As you lift your arms, stretch your knees.

6 For the first "hopsa" put your weight on your right leg and hop lightly. At the second "hopsa" move the same way but with your left leg, etc. Immediately continue with 7.

7 Jump with both feet together and arms up as in 5 and 6. Support the jump with your lifted arms and bounce with your knees.

8 As in 6.
9 With arms up, turn around once during the three "trallalas." Each time, at the

	first "a" in "trallala," step with your right foot. On the last "a," step with your left foot while pulling up the knee of your inactive leg.
10 Hopsa-hopsa! 　　Hopsassa! Hopsassa! 　　　　　　Hopsassa! 　　Hopsa-hopsa! 　　Trallala! Trallala! Trallala!	10 Repeat the bunny dance as in 6 – 9.
11 Pricks up his ears –	11 As in 4.
12 listens –	12 Turn your head in all directions and "listen." Make sure your gesture makes clear that you listen, not stare. Staring will frighten sensitive children.
13 runs a pace –	13 Return to the bunny position as in 1.
14 Hop-hop,	14 Jump into space with two or more large jumps with feet closed.
15 to his hiding-place!	15 At "hiding-place," crouch behind a chair, curtain or table. If you play outside, hide behind a bush or rock. Crouch deep enough so that your chin is between your knees, your elbows on the sides of your knees. The hands are still against the forehead as "bunny ears." The bunny makes himself as small as possible.
16 Sits quite still.	16 Remain crouched.
17 With his big, long ears	17 Lift your head and upper body a little, stretching your fingers as ears a little more.
18 can hear	18 Move your hands down behind your own ears to help you hear better. See illustration at left.

19 That the fox is coming near.
    Quiet movement

20 Sits quiet as a mouse.
    Quiet-as-a-mouse.
21 Listens –
22 looks –

23 fox went away.

24 Bunny is alone –

25 hurray!

26 Sits again in the grass,
    Nose in the air, sniff, sniff.

VARIATION I:

18 can hear:
19a bow – wow –
        ⌐   ⌐
            bow-wow - wow
          ⌐   ⌐   ⌐
    that the dog is coming near
          ⌐   ⌐

19 With your right hand, rest your stretched middle and ring fingers on your stretched thumb. Pointer and pinky, also stretched, are lifted slightly as "fox ears." The fox comes sneaking from the right hip along the side of your right thigh, around your knees and again along the side of the left thigh, not further then midthigh. The fox sneaks silently.

20 Take on the bunny crouch again, as in 15.
21 As in 18.
22 Assume bunny position as in 1. Look very alert to right and left as you make a few steps forward.
23 The bunny looks straight ahead while shaking his head.
24 As in 23, but this time nod your head gladly.
25 With arms held high the bunny makes a jump, then returns to his former position.
26 As in 1 and 2.

19a Your right hand forms the dog's nose: all four fingers lie stretched next to each other. Your thumb is the "lower jaw," its upper joint resting on the middle joint of your middle finger (see the illustration.) At "bow-wow," your fingers, still

If you want to extend the game with the dog and/or the hunter, follow point 26 with the repetition from points, 3 to 18 (including the repeat of the dance from 6 to 9.) Repeat text and movement without changes. Starting at 19a, use the text at left. The text and movements for the hunter are shown in Variation II.

113

VARIATION II:

18 can hear
19b that the hunter
    o-o
            is coming near.

CONCLUSION:

27 Snuggles (sits down) in
            a grassy nest,
   In the shining sun
            must rest.
   Comes a gentle wind
            so mild,
   Sings softly for my
            bunny child.

close together and stretched, move up from your thumb: the dog opens his mouth, but shuts it again right away. Do the movements rhythmically, as marked.

19b For the hunter, each hand makes a circle with pointer and thumb; your other fingers are held tightly together. Look through these circles as if they were binoculars.

27 Resting can be done in various ways:
If you have played within a circle of stools, each bunny returns to his or her stool. If you played freely in your play space, the bunnies lie down on the floor. You also lie down with them, singing softly the Wind-soo-soo song, pg. 115. You could also walk from child to child and gently wave a delicate wind over each with a reed fan or some other suitable material. The children enjoy the gentle air and relax in the quiet surrounding them.

Here you can hum or sing the Wind-soo-soo.

When you want to close the game, follow 26 with Conclusion.

Wind-soo-soo

Quietly floating and swinging   *Text and Melody: Wilma Ellersiek*

Sings the wind   mild   for the   bun-ny   child

Soo-soo-soo! Soo-soo-soo! Soo_, Soo_, Soo_ Soo_!!
Soo-soo-soo! Soo-soo-soo! Soo_, Soo_, Soo_ Soo_!

Notation: ● ≈ one pulsation (basic unit) / ⊘ ≈ ●● /
○ ≈ ●●●● / (: :) ≈ repeat / ⊘ ⊘ ≈ sustain / ~ ≈ sustain longer
/ ﹏﹏ ≈ die out, at the same time slower and softer
/ ⌒ ≈ phrase

The Little Fish
Small Rhythmic-Musical Story

IN THE LIVELY WATER WAVES
A LITTLE FISH IS SWIMMING.

SWIMS – SWIMS – SWIMS,
SPRINGS – DIVES – SPLASHES
AND RESTS.

SWIMS – SWIMS – SWIMS,
SPRINGS – DIVES – SPLASHES
AND RESTS.

IS SWINGING, SWINGING WITH THE WAVES,
Silent movement
SWINGING – SWINGING – SWINGING.

TEXT:

1. In the lively water waves

2. A little fish is swimming.

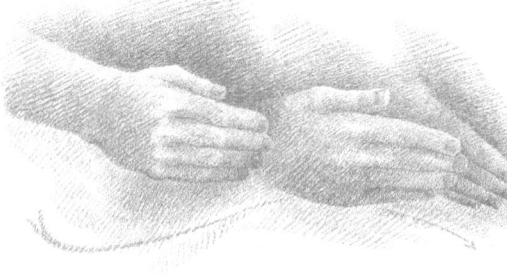

HAND GESTURES:

1. Holding your hands next to each other, horizontally, with palms down, make wave movements up and down from left to right at about the height of your stomach.

2. Your right hand is the "fish." Your palm is turned toward your body, the edge of your pinky toward the floor. Coming from the right side, the fish swims in a wavy line until it is in front of you. While swimming, your right hand must be as flexible as the body of a little trout. As you move, your fingers lightly bend and stretch. At the same time, make a slight rolling

Your hand is not meant to be a realistic picture of the little fish. Rather, the task is to show and experience the various movement possibilities in the water: swimming back and forth, springing, diving, resting and rocking.

3	Swims – swims – swims,	3	The fish swims from left to right in the backward direction, leading with the right wrist. Speak very melodiously, almost singing.
4	Springs – dives – splashes	4	For "springs," push your hand vertically upward, higher than your head, while speaking dynamically in a high voice. Before "dives," turn your hand, still above your head, with your fingertips facing downward. Then, still speaking dynamically in a darker voice, push your hand down to your knee, and then in a curve up to chest level. Now spread the fingers of your right hand and at "splashes," whirl your hand and lower arm in a very lively way.
5	And rests.	5	Close the fingers of your right hand again and hold your hand very still in front of you, speaking the word "rests" in a soft, dark tone.
6	Swims – swims – swims, Springs – dives – splashes And rests.	6	Repeat as in 3, 4 and 5.
7	Is swinging, swinging with the waves,	7	From the position of rest, led by your right elbow, the fish rocks back and forth in place. Your right hand is relaxed, and passively allows the rocking movement. Speak rhythmically, but still very melodiously.

(continued from previous page: movement with your lower arm as it moves up and down. The movement starts at the fingertips.)

8   *Silent*

8   Continue the rocking movement for a while without speech, looking attentively and lovingly at the little fish.

9   Swinging – swinging – swinging.

9   Quietly go on rocking while moving your hand to the left, speaking in a sing-song voice until your hand cannot rock any further. Then slowly let your arm sink and still look after it silently for a little while.

The Doggy Tapple-Tapples
Rhythmic-Musical Hand Gesture Game

"Bow-wow – bow-wow – bow-wow,"
Barks the doggy now: "Bow-wow."
He tapples: tipple-tapple-tapple,
Tipple-tapple-tapple-tips – then sits.

Lifts his paw for you to take,
Plays a trick: Here doggy, shake –
Doggy, shake – doggy, shake!
And sits back down quick.

Yes, for this trick
Give him a sausage, quick,
Here! Snap! Nap-nap!
And a little bowl
Of water to lick.

Lappy-lappy-lappy-lappy – lappy-lappy-lappy-lappy –
Lappy-lappy-lappy-lappy – lappy-lappy-lappy-lap.

The bowl is empty now.
The doggy lifts his taili-o
And wags and wags it to and fro.

Wiggle-wiggle-waggle-waggle –
Wiggle-wiggle-tackle-tackle –
Wiggle-wiggle-waggle-waggle –
Wiggle-wiggle-tackle-tack!
This means: "Thank you," I think,
"Thank you, thanks for food and drink!"

"Bow-wow – bow-wow – bow-wow,"
Barks the doggy now: "Bow-wow."
He tapples: tipple-tapple-tip,
Tapples round the corner quick.

TEXT:	GESTURES

1 "Bow-wow – bow-wow –
  ∠ ∠   ∠ ∠
         bow-wow,"
           ∠ ∠

	1 Your right hand forms the dog's "nose" with all four fingers stretched and lying next to each other. Your thumb is the "lower jaw," its upper joint resting on the middle joint of your middle finger. See illustration. At each " ∠ " open and close the "mouth," alternating small and wide: " ∠ , ∠ ." Speak softer or louder, according to the movement. Pause after the last "wow."

2 Barks the doggy now:
  ∠ ∠ ∠ ∠
         "Bow-wow."
           ∠ ∠
	2 Continue barking rhythmically, with the given accents.

3 He tapples:
     tipple-tapple-tapple –,
     o o o o o
 Tipple-tapple-tapple-tips –
 o o o o o o
	3 Set the pointer and middle finger of your right hand lightly on your thigh, as "paws." With the hand-movement, try to imitate the flexible steps of a dog. The doggy runs once around in a circle, each "*o*" shows a step of his paw.

4 Then sits.	4 At "sits," roll all of your fingers into a fist, and emphatically put your fist down on your right thigh.
5 Lifts his paw for you to take,	5 As a transition from a hand gesture to a large gesture, lift your lower arms up, leaving your hands hanging down loosely as paws.

6 Plays a trick: Here,
           doggy, shake –
 Doggy, shake –
           doggy, shake!
	6 Lift your right paw lightly and move it forward at "shake," as if to shake hands. Bring your paw

			back to the original position, then repeat the movement twice. Your left paw moves along with the right. Pay attention when saying the three identical words: be sure to vary the speech melody.
7	And sits back down quick.	7	Dissolve the paw gesture; lower your arms while making fists with your hands and lay them down on your thighs, close to your knees.

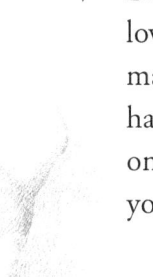

8	Yes,	8	Lift your left lower arm and stick up your pointer. Your right hand remains lying on your thigh, unchanged.
9	For this trick	9	Lightly incline your left pointer forwards, to emphasize your words, and also nod at "this." Then your pointer disappears.
10	Give him a sausage, quick.	10	At the word "sausage," stick your left thumb out horizontally from your fist. Your rolled-in fingers face the children: the back of your hand faces yourself. Lift the sausage a little so it can be easily seen.
11	Here!	11	With the word: "here," move the sausage toward the doggy. At the same time, your right fist, still lying on your thigh, becomes the doggie's mouth. See gesture at 1.

12 Snap!

12 The doggy snaps at the sausage in a quick movement. As soon as the mouth closes, let your thumb disappear into your left fist, also bringing down your left arm and letting it hang at your side next to your thigh. However, concentrate on your right hand.

13 Nap-nap!

13 At each "nap," the doggy opens and shuts his mouth. He is eating the sausage.

14 And a little bowl of
    water to lick.

14 Form a bowl with your left hand and set it on your left thigh. During this time your right hand still holds the doggy mouth gesture.

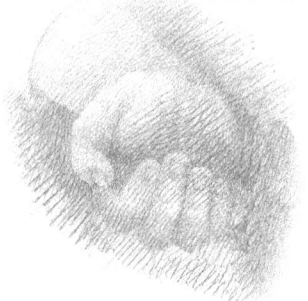

15 Lappy-lappy-lappy-lappy –
    lappy-lappy-lappy-lappy –

Lappy-lappy-lappy-lappy -
    lappy-lappy-lappy-lap.

15 Your right hand also forms a bowl: the "tongue," held at a right angle with your fingertips above your left hand. For the lapping, roll up your fingers and stretch them again rhythmically. Don't speak the "lappy-lappy" too fast. This will ensure that the fingers of your right hand can be exact in doing the rolling movement at each "a."

16 The bowl is empty now.

16 Show the empty water bowl to the children. Your right hand hangs down without a gesture. Then dissolve the bowl gesture and pause.

17 The doggy lifts his taili-o

17 Lift your right fist up to about stomach height and at the word: "taili-o," stick up your thumb.

18 And wags and wags it
   ↖ ↗
              to and fro.
              ↖ ↗
   Wiggle-wiggle-
   ↖ ↗
              waggle-waggle –
              ↖ ↗
   Wiggle-wiggle-
   ↖ ↗
              tackle-tackle –
              ↖ ↗
   Wiggle-wiggle-
   ↖ ↗
              waggle-waggle –
              ↖ ↗
   Wiggle-wiggle-tackle-tack!
   ↖ ↗ ↖ ↗ ↖ ↗

19 This means: "Thank you,"
   ↖ ↗
              I think,
              ↖ ↗
   "Thank you, thanks for
   ↖ ↗ ↖ ↗
              food and drink!"
              ↖ ↗

20 "Bow-wow – bow-wow –
   ∠   ∠   ∠   ∠
              bow-wow,"
              ∠   ∠
   Barks the doggy now:
   ∠   ∠   ∠ ∠
              "Bow-wow."
              ∠   ∠

21 He tapples:
   o o o
              tapple-tapple-tip –
              o o o o o

22 Tapples round the
   o   o   o   o
              corner quick.
              o   o

18 Wag the "taili-o" in the speech rhythm. Only your thumb moves! Your fist remains still.

19 At: "This means" and "I think" lift the "taili-o" a little and wag twice as fast.

20 Quickly change the wagging gesture into the "dog mouth" and bark as in 1.

21 Quickly change the mouth gesture: your pointer and middle finger stand as paws on your thigh and tapple toward your hip in the flexible dog walk.

22 Continue to tapple, and after the last word the doggy will disappear behind your back.

The Honey Bee
Rhythmic-Musical Hand Gesture Game

FROM THE HIVE, A BEE – ZZZZ – ZZZZ –
FLIES OUT HAPPILY.

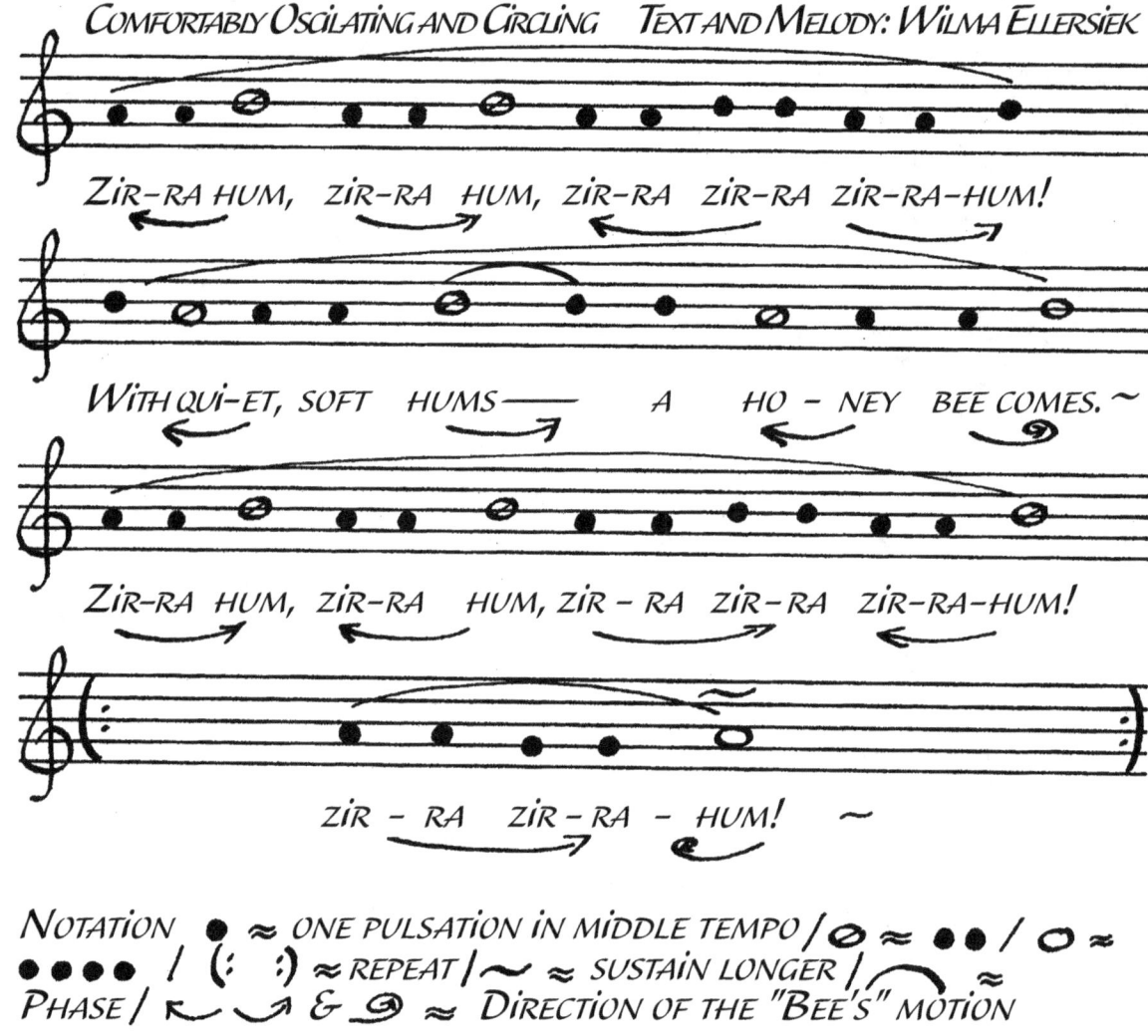

THE BEE FLIES TO THE FLOWER BRIGHT.
ZZZZZZT!
STICKS HER TRUNK DEEP INSIDE,
HFFFFFF – SUCKS,
HFFFFFF – SUCKS NECTAR RIGHT.
ZIRRA-HUM, ZIRRA-HUM, ZIRRA-ZIRRA-ZIRRA-HUM,
THE BEE FLIES TO THE NEXT FLOWER BRIGHT,
HFFFFFF – SUCKS,
HFFFFFF – SUCKS NECTAR RIGHT.

Zirra-hum, zirra-hum, zirra-zirra-zirra-hum,
To the beehive flies the honey bee,
Slips inside and rests, and rests, does she.
Zzzz – zzzz – zzzz!

TEXT:	HAND GESTURES:

TEXT:

1. From the hive,
   a bee – zzzz – zzzz –

2. Flies out happily.

3. *Song:*
   Zirra-hum, zirra-hum,
      zirra-hum, zirra-hum!
   With quiet, soft hums
      a honey bee comes.
   Zirra-hum, zirra-hum,
      zirra-hum, zirra-hum!
   Zirra-zirra-hum!

HAND GESTURES:

1. Form a "hive" with your lower arms. Your flat hands lie on top of each other, with the palm of your left hand resting on the back of your right hand. With your right ear bend down to the hive so that your can hear the humming. You create this humming at the same time, by a voiced "zzzz-zzzz."

2. Your right hand becomes the "bee." Your left arm remains in the position of the hive. For the bee, stick out your pointer from your lightly formed fist. The bee flies in an arc out of the hive. Then begin to sing the Zirra-hum song.

3. During the song, the honey bee rocks and circles through the air as noted with arrows underneath the song text. At the song's last tone, the bee flies in a circle and, at the same time, your left hand forms a "blossom," to which the bee then flies.

4   The bee flies to
            the flower bright.

4   The bee flies in a loop, as shown at right, close to the blossom.

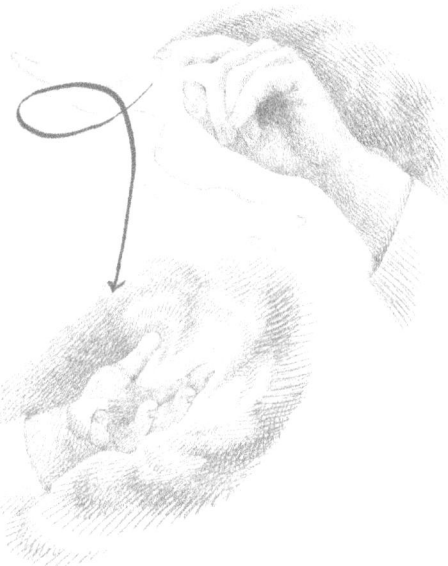

5   Zzzzzzt!

5   The honey bee flies very close to the blossom and with the "t" of the "zzzzt," sits down on its rim.

6   Sticks her trunk deep inside,

6   The bee dips the right pointer, its trunk, into the blossom.

7   Hffffff – sucks,
     Hffffff – sucks nectar right.

7   To sound the "hfffff," form your lips as if to say "u" (as in hurt). Then suck air through your lips. As long as the "hfffff" sounds, pull the "trunk" slightly from the middle of the blossom: the bee sucks in the nectar. At the word "sucks," dip the trunk back. Repeat. Then lift the trunk at the word "nectar."

8   Zirra-hum, zirra-hum,
           zirra-zirra-zirra-hum,
   The bee flies to
         the next flower bright,

8   The bee flies away from the blossom and rocks in arcs through the air. Then repeat 5 - 7. (This process can again be repeated or you can pass on to 9.)

Hffffff – sucks,
Hffffff – sucks nectar right.

9 Zirra-hum, zirra-hum,
zirra-zirra-zirra-hum,
To the beehive flies
the huney bee,

9 With the marked rocking movements the honey bee starts to return home. At the word "beehive," the bee circles in a large loop, while the left arm forms the hive.

10 Slips inside and rests,
and rests, does she.
Zzzz – zzzz – zzzz!

10 At the word "inside," the bee slips under the left hand. Dissolve the bee gesture and complete the hive with your right lower arm. Listen to the humming of the bees with your right ear. Slowly dissolve your gesture.

The Little Bear
Rhythmic-Musical Hand Gesture Game

"Grumm – grumm."
Grummel-grumm, the little bear,
Dop-dop-dop-dop-dop-dop-dop,
Plods through the woods to the honey tree.
"Bzzzz-bzzz – bzzzzzzz!"

Honey sweet to get at quick,
Honey sweet he hopes to lick.
"Hmmm – hmmm!"

"Bzzzz-bzzz – bzzzzzzz!"
The bees come flying: "Bzzzzzzz!"
They want to sting – to sting:
"Zzzzzt – zzzzt – zzzzt – zzzzt!"
The bear cub, the fresh thing.

He hardly notices the prick
For, to his luck, his coat is thick.
"Bzzzz-bzzz – bzzzzzzz!"

"Bzzzz-bzzz – bzzzzzzz!"
From buzz and hum
His head feels numb.
"Bzzzz-bzzz – bzzzzzzz!"
"Bzzzz-bzzz – bzzzzzzz!"

Runs as fast as he can
Dop-dop-dop-dop.
Back home to his den.
Dop-dop-dop-dop-dop-dop-dop.

At home he feels right
And can rest from his fright.
"Grumm – grumm."
Can rest.

TEXT:	HAND GESTURES:

1   "Grumm – grumm."
    Grummel-grumm,
          the little bear,
	1 Sit heavily on a chair or stool, feeling yourself to be a bear. Hold your hands in front of your chest, as paws, and rhythmically rock from side to side. The rocking is a weight transfer in the bones of your seat, not just from your waist.

2   Dop-dop-dop-dop-dop-
    r   l   r   l   r
          dop-dop,
          l   r
  Plods through the woods
    l   r   l   r
	2 Dissolve your paw position and plod with your flat hands along your thighs in a "bear walk." Start close to your upper body, and with eleven steps plod up to your knees. Support the plodding with a light rocking movement created by weight transfer.

3 to the honey tree. 	3 Form a "hive" with your lower arms and your flat hands lying on top of each other. Your left hand rests with the palm on the back of your right hand.
4 "Bzzzz-bzzz – bzzzzzzz!"	4 With your right ear bend down to the hive so that your can hear the humming. You create this humming at the same moment by a voiced "bzzzz-bzzz."

5   Honey sweet to get
          at quick,
  Honey sweet he hopes
          to lick.
  "Hmmm – hmmm!"
	5 With your hands, pretend to carry a small tray and move it towards you (the bear fetches the honey). The movement is comfortably slow so that

6 "Bzzzz-bzz – bzzzzzzz!"
   ⌣⌣⌣ ⌒ ⌒
   / r / r / r
   The bees come flying:
   ⌣⌣⌣
   / r / r
                    "bzzzzzzz!"
                      ⌒ ⌒
                      / r

6 Stick out your pointers from both of your loose fists; your fingertips are the "bees." Sound the humming with a voiced "zzz." The bees fly away from each other, toward each other, and in an arc from the outside and above back to the starting position; see the arrows under the text. Repeat the whole movement.

7 They want to sting –
                ↑
                      to sting:
                            ↑
   "Zzzzzt – zzzzt – zzzzt –
      ↑   ↑   ↑
                            zzzzt!"
                               ↑

7 Holding your pointers parallel, fingertips pointing to the children, push them forward as marked. Here the "z" is very sharply pronounced and ends in a hard "t." The bees sting!

8 The bear cub,
            the fresh thing.

8 The bear sits as in 1, without moving. He nods only at "fresh."

9 He hardly notices
     ← →
               the prick
                 ← →

9 The bear still sits without moving, he only shakes his head "no," at the words underlined with arrows.

---

at the words "get at," your wrists are close to your mouth. At "quick" and "lick," move your hands down from your wrists to your fingertips, as if to lick them. Sound the "l" in "lick" for a while and, while doing so, stick out your tongue. At "Hmmm – hmmm," lick your hands twice more while sounding a comfortable "hmmm."

10 For, to his luck,

      .. ..

           his coat is thick.

               .. ..

11 "Bzzzz-bzzz – bzzzzzzz!"

      / r / r   /   r

   "Bzzzz-bzzz – bzzzzzzz!"

      / r / r   /   r

12 From buzz and hum

13 His head feels numb.

14 "Bzzzz-bzzz – bzzzzzzz!"

      / r / r   /   r

   "Bzzzz-bzzz – bzzzzzzz!"

      / r / r   /   r

15 Runs as fast as he can

16 Dop-dop-dop-dop.

    .   .   .   .

    r / r /

   Back home to his den.

    .   .   .   .

    r / r /

   Dop-dop-dop-dop-

    .   .   .   .

    r / r /

        dop-dop-dop-dop.

        .   .   .   .

        r / r /

10 Now the bear slaps his body with his flat hands – first his chest, then his stomach, his belly and lastly, his thighs. Slap with both paws at the same time, while shaking your head "no." Allow yourself lots of time for the slapping and speak the text slowly.

11 Quickly change from bear to bees. Move as in 6.

12 As they hum, the bees fly circles around your ears.

13 Now as the bear, hold your ears shut with your paws (flat hands.)

14 As in 6.

15 As a bear in the bear position, lift your paws above your head.

16 As in 2. His speed becomes noticeably faster, but he must make very small steps so as to stay within the distance from body to knees.

17 At home he feels right

18 And can rest from
           his fright.

19 "Grumm – grumm."

20 Can rest.

17 A little above your forehead lay your lower arms on top of each other, bending your head slightly.

18 Slowly lower your arms; then, move as in 1. Sit this way for a while.

19 This time the bear moves gently forward and back.

20 Sit quietly in the bear position, hanging your head down in front of you.

So Runs My Pony
Rhythmic-Musical Movement Game

My pony runs:
Hop-hop – hop-hop,
Gallopp-gallopp – hop-hop – hop-hop,
Gallopp-gallopp – gallopp-gallopp,
Hop-hop – hop-hop – hop-hop – hop-hop.

He trots: trot – trotta - trot – trotta,
Trot-trot – trotta – trot-trot-trot,
Trot-trot – trotta – trotta – trotta,
Trot-trot-trot-trot-trot-trot-trot.

Whoa!
My pony stops so,
On he doesn't want to go.

He huffs: phrrr! – phrrr!
And puffs: pfff – pfff!
Pfff – pfff – pfffff!

And rests. And rests.

TEXT:

1   My pony runs:
    Hop-hop – hop-hop,
    Gallopp-gallopp –
        hop-hop – hop-hop,
    Gallopp-gallopp –
        gallopp-gallopp,
    Hop-hop – hop-hop –
        hop-hop – hop-hop.

MOVEMENTS:

1   This game needs plenty of room for the "ponies" to move. At the beginning, stand in the room, with your head slightly lowered. Try to express in your posture the character of a pony in its posture. In galloping, bend your knees well, so that each jump portrays something of the strength of a pony. It is best to move in a clockwise direction in order to avoid collisions. Your speech must be

2 He trots: trot – trot –
              trotta – trotta,
   Trot-trot – trotta –
              trot-trot-trot,
   Trot-trot – trotta –
              trotta – trotta,
   Trot-trot-trot-trot-
              trot-trot-trot.

3 Whoa!
   My pony stops so,
   On he doesn't want to go.
        ←   →   ←

powerful; the galloping must be jolly and fast in accord with the children's short legs. After the end of the gallop-text, allow the movement to turn into trotting, without speaking. Once you have achieved the slower trotting step, continue with the text.

2 Again, while trotting, lift your knees well and find a speed fitting the children. Your voice need not be as powerful as during the galloping; instead, make sure that your speech melody varies. Continue moving clockwise, slowing down at the last line of the text.

3 Call: "Whoa!" while still taking the last slow steps. Start the "whoa!" strongly, then let it sound dark and soft. Stop and look to make sure that all the children have stopped too. Otherwise, repeat the "whoa!" Only when all children have stopped, continue with the line: "The pony stops so, on he doesn't want to go." The pony shakes his head: "no," as shown by the arrows.

4 He huffs: phrrr! – phrrr!
   And puffs: pfff – pfff!
   Pfff – pfff – pfffff!

5 And rests. And rests.

4 For the huff: "phrrrrr!" blow the air through your completely relaxed lips, so that they vibrate. For the puff: "pfff," blow the air in a directed stream through your lips, without vibrating.

5 Stand quietly with a slightly bent head for a little while. From this point the game can be repeated once or twice. Several possibilities may be used for the ending.

Further play suggestions:

I He gallops no more,
          far or near,
   He stays at home,
   At home – right here.

I Gently stroke all the children over head, neck and back. You need not continue the verse during the whole time. The children will have a stronger experience when it is very quiet some of the time.

or:

II My pony runs no
          more ahead,
    He lies down on a
          grassy bed,
    And rests instead.
    And I shall sing (blow)
          with you
    A calming Diddledoo.
    Let us ask the mild
          wind here:
    Sing "loo-loo" for
          pony dear.

II Before you speak the words: "lies down," quickly bend your knees, kneel down while supporting yourself with your hands and then lie down on your side with bent knees. When all ponies lie quietly, say with a soft, dark voice: "and I sing…" and then start the *Rest-Diddledoo* or *Blow, Blow, Wind so Mild* song—singing or humming. You could also play the melody on a Choroi-flute, substituting "blow" for "sing."

Rest Diddledoo
For Choroi Flute

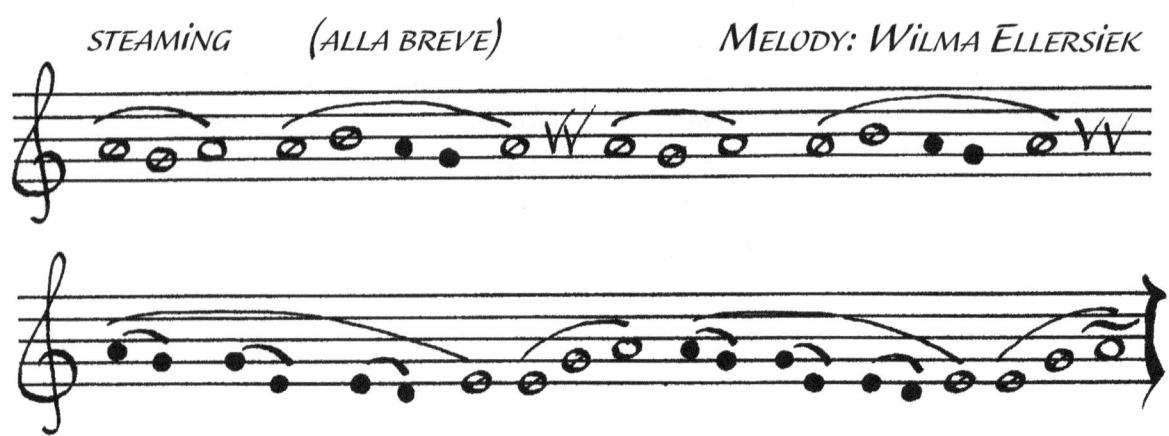

Blow Wind, Blow So Mild

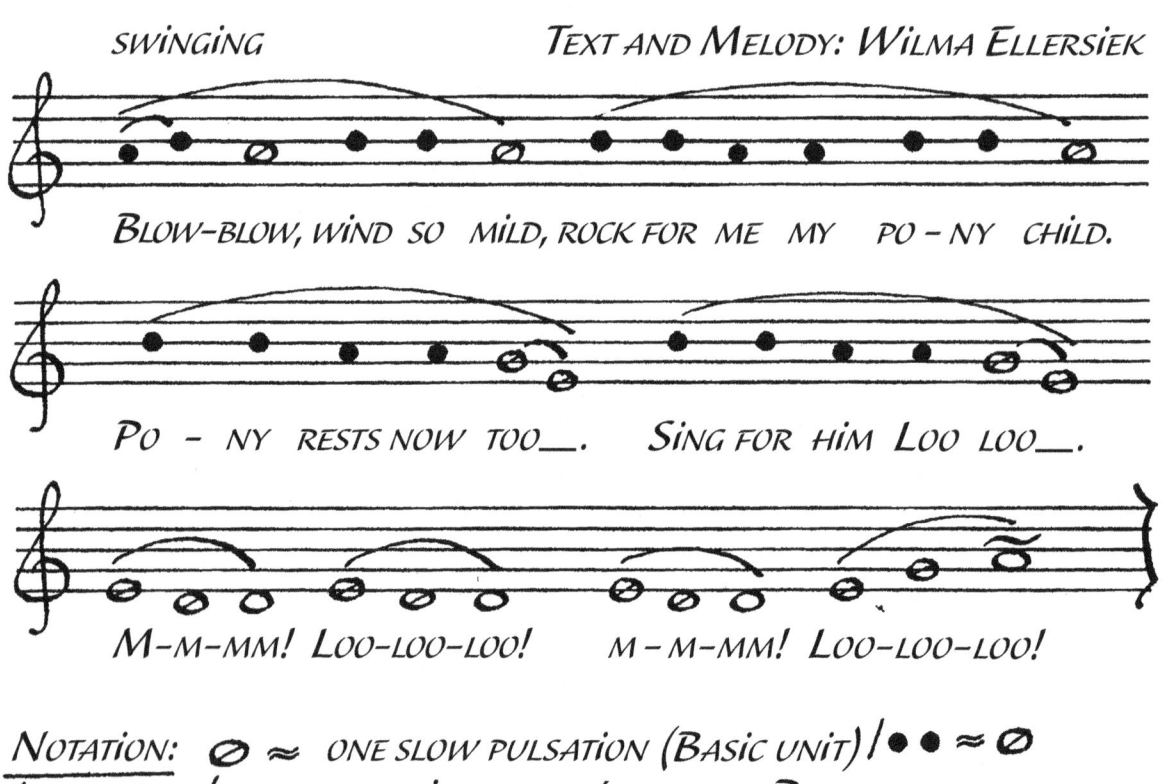

or:

III My pony runs no more ahead,
He slowly walks into his shed:
Step-step-step-step,
And he's nodding with his head.
Step-step-step-step,
And he's nodding with his head.
Lays himself upon the straw,
So-so – so-soh!

III At "no more," shake your head. Speak the sentence: "he slowly walks into his shed" while still standing, then slowly start to walk. Again pull up your knees high and step on the ground toes first. At the same time nod your head with each step. At: "lays himself upon the straw," lie down as described in II. Sing one of the lullabies at the end.

After the basic game has been played two or three times, a further way to express the movement of the pony may be added:

The Little Donkey
Rhythmic-Musical Movement Game

THE DONKEY FOAL, "HEE-HAW! HEE-HAW! HEE-HA-AW!"
PAWS WITH HIS LEG –
SCRAPY-SCRAPY-SCRAPY-SCRAPE –
AND TROTS ALONG WITH GENTLE STEP:

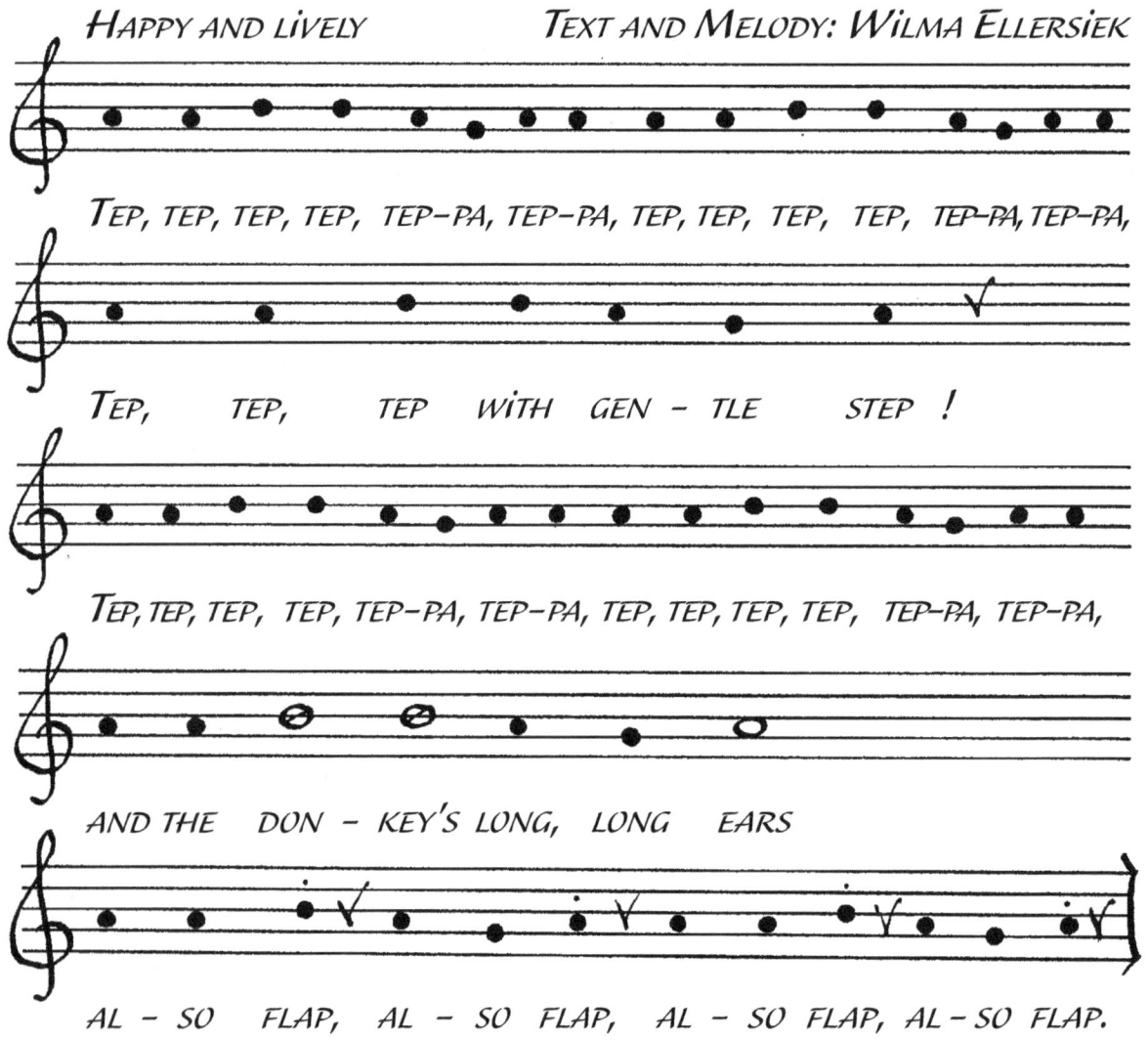

Happy and lively — Text and Melody: Wilma Ellersiek

TEP, TEP, TEP, TEP, TEP-PA, TEP-PA, TEP, TEP, TEP, TEP, TEP-PA, TEP-PA,
TEP, TEP, TEP WITH GEN - TLE STEP!
TEP, TEP, TEP, TEP, TEP-PA, TEP-PA, TEP, TEP, TEP, TEP, TEP-PA, TEP-PA,
AND THE DON - KEY'S LONG, LONG EARS
AL - SO FLAP, AL - SO FLAP, AL - SO FLAP, AL - SO FLAP.

NOTATION ● ≈ ONE PULSATION (BASIC UNIT) | ⊘ ≈ ● ● | ⦵ ≈ ● ● ● ●
⋅● ≈ ONE STACCATTO PULSATION | ✓ ≈ PAUSE OF ONE BASIC UNIT.

THE DONKEY STANDS AND CALLS: "HEE-HAW,"
HEE-HAW! HEE-HAW! HEE-HA-AW!"
THEN CLIMBS THE MOUNTAIN FAR.

Slowly – slowly – step by step,
Step – step – step – step
Step – step – step by step
And the ears go flap, flap, flap.

Steep – steep – steep – steep –
Up he goes without a stop.
Finally he is on top.
Stops and calls: "Hee-haw! Hee-haw!"
Huffs: Puhhhh! Puhhhh! Puhhhhfff!
Puhhhh! Puhhhhfff! Puhhhhfff!

There – now it is time to go.
But the donkey just stands so.
Headstrong and quite without par
And calls: "Hee-ha-aw! Hee-ha-a-aw!"

With crooked ears stands still.
No-no, it's not his will,
No – no – no!
Calls: "Hee-ha-aw!" No, he does not
Want to move from this high spot.

Headstrong, he stands quite still,
To move is not his will.
My donkey wants to rest,
He lies down in the grass to rest
Down in the grass is best.

Rest-fifth: It is enough!

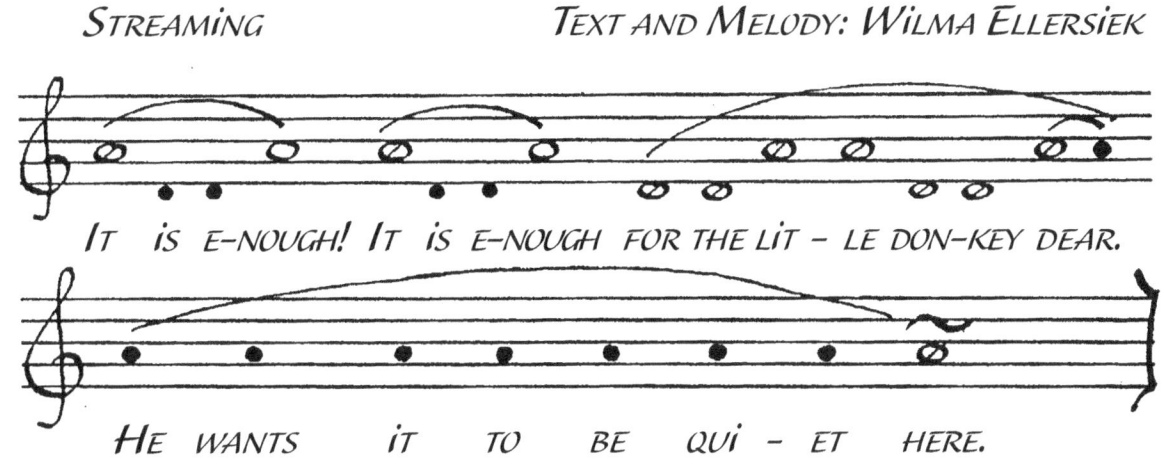

Streaming — Text and Melody: Wilma Ellersiek

It is e-nough! It is e-nough for the lit-tle don-key dear.
He wants it to be qui-et here.

Comes a gentle wind,
Phhhh! – Phhhh!
Softly strokes – soft and mild
Phhhh! – Phhhh!
The hide of the donkey child.
Phhhh! – Phhhh!
Softly strokes – soft and mild
Phhhh! – Phhhh!
The hide of the donkey child.
Phhhh! – Phhhh! – Phhhhhhh!

The donkey, he has rested now!
Stretches – stretches –
Rolls all around –
Gets up and stands
On his legs again.
Rested now! Rested now!
The donkey stands and calls out free:
"Hee-haw! Hee-ha-aw!" So happily!

TEXT:	MOVEMENTS:

1 The donkey foal,
     "Hee-haw! – Hee-haw! –
       Hee-Ha-aw!"
	1 Stand upright with your neck slightly bent. Your hands, palms to the children, fingers and thumbs tightly closed and stretched to the fingertips, lie with the balls of your thumbs against the side of your forehead as "donkey's ears." At: "Hee-haw! – Hee-ha-aw!" stretch at the middle of your body upwards at "Hee," and at the "haw," relax again, back to your starting position. The donkey's call should not be naturalistic; it should be musical and

2 Paws with his leg: —
   ≢   ≢ ≢ ‥
   Scrapy-scrapy-scrapy-scrape
   ≢ ≢ ≢ ≢

2 In the same position, scrape across the floor with the ball of your right foot from front to back at each "≢." After the third time, once again set both feet, one after the other, firmly on the floor. Remove the ear gesture. Hold your hands against your upper chest, like "paws." Then continue to scrape four more times in the given rhythm.

3 And trots along with
        r / r /
              gentle step: -
              r / r /
   Tep, tep, tep, tep,
      r / r /
              teppa-teppa, etc.
              r / r /

3 Draw out the word "and"; it is the place where you begin trotting. Lift your knee noticably and begin trotting clockwise in light steps. It is important for you to trot lightly and not too fast. Even as you trot, try to keep you head in the characteristic head position of a donkey. Starting with "tep, tep, tep," begin singing while you trot.

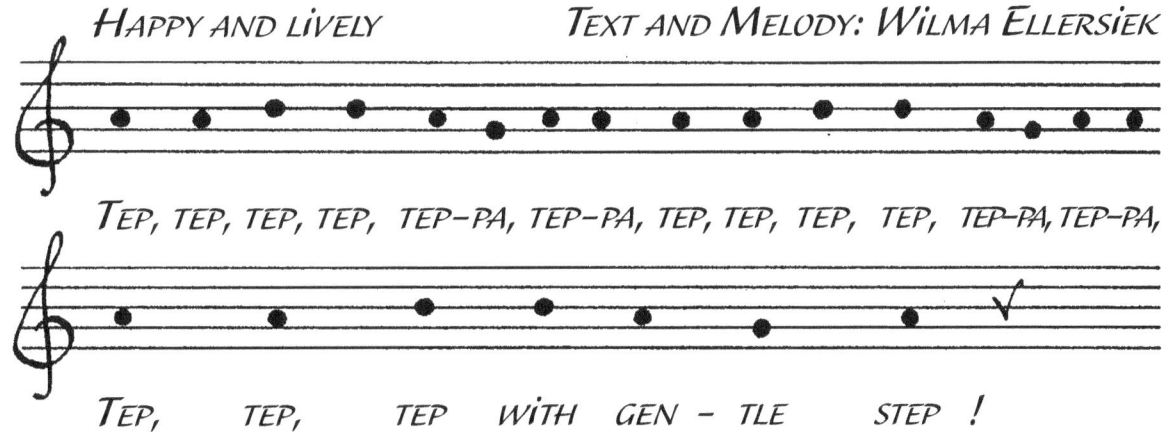

Happy and lively   Text and Melody: Wilma Ellersiek

Tep, tep, tep, tep, tep-pa, tep-pa, tep, tep, tep, tep, tep-pa, tep-pa,

Tep, tep, tep with gen - tle step !

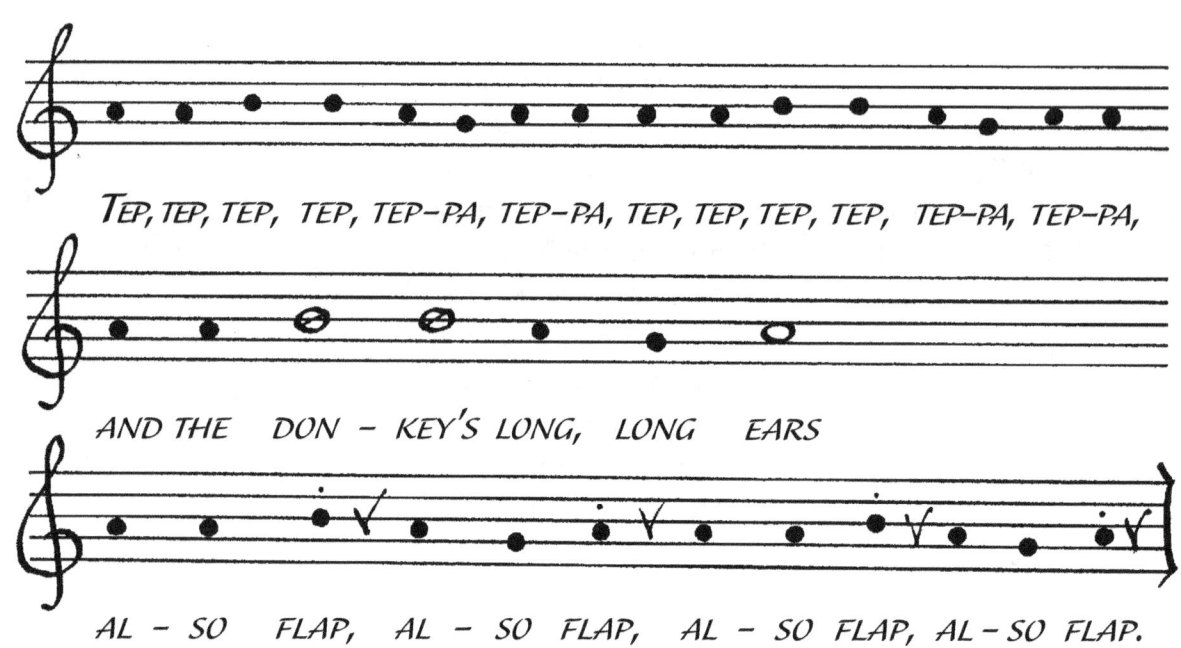

NOTATION ● ≈ ONE PULSATION (BASIC UNIT) | ○ ≈ ●● | ○ ≈ ●●●●
ᛠ ≈ ONE STACCATO PULSATION | ˇ ≈ PAUSE OF ONE BASIC UNIT.

4 And the donkey's long,
  　　　　long ears

5 Also flap, also flap,
  ↓ ↑ ↓ ↑
  　　　also flap, also flap.
  　　　↓ ↑ ↓ ↑

6 The donkey stands and calls:
  "He-haw! Hee-haw!
  　　　　Hee-ha-aw!"

7 Then climbs the
  　　　mountain far.

4 Still singing, stop trotting at "and the donkey's." At "long, long ears" dissolve the paw gesture and form ears again as in 1.

5 At "al" in "also," nod as you bend your fingertips forward, and at "flap" revert to the original position with your head straight. Do this four times. After the last tone, pause briefly.

6 With upright ears stand in the characteristic donkey position for a short while, calling "Hee-haw" in a fifth interval, and stretch your middle as in 1.

7 Dissolve ear gestures and return to the paw position.

8 Slowly – slowly –
           r   /
               step by step,
             r   /
   Step – step – step – step
    r   /   r   /
   Step – step – step by step
    r   /   r   /

9 And the ears go
            flap, flap, flap.

10 Steep – steep –
      r   /
          steep – steep –
             r   /
   Up he goes without a stop.
    r   /   r   /
   (continue walking silently)
    r   /   r   /

11 Finally he is on top.
      r   /

12 Stops and calls:
      "Hee-haw! Hee-haw!"
13 Huffs:
   Puhhhh! Puhhhh!
   Puhhhhfff!
   Puhhhh! Puhhhhfff!
              Puhhhhfff!

14 There – now it is time
                  to go.

15 But the donkey just
      stands so.

8 "Climb the mountain" in heavy, comfortable steps, flexible in the knees, but don't stamp. Hold your head slightly down.

9 Continue climbing, but form ears again and allow them to nod rhythmically.

10 Again form paws. The little donkey is getting tired and moves a little more slowly. Don't slow too much, however. The children must be able to imitate the stalking tempo. Instead, increase the rocking in the knees. The size of the steps, however, should remain the same.

11 At "finally," and "on top," make two last, slow steps. The donkey, his head hanging down, comes to a stop.

12 As in 1.

13 At "huffs," take a deep breath and with "puhhhh" silently blow out your breath, holding your head low. Let your lips vibrate at "puhff" for the "ff". The huffing may be repeated.

14 At the word "there," form paws again and at "to go," look in confirmation at the children.

15 Remain standing without movement, head bent and hands as paws.

Here text and movements of 8 and 9 may be repeated, or continue with 10.

16 Headstrong and quite
   ‿‿
               without par
       ‿‿

17 And calls:
   "Hee-ee-haw! Hee-ee-haw!"
18 With crooked ears
               stands still.

16 Pull your head in a little as if you would push with your forehead. At "headstrong and without par" lightly bend your knees twice. The donkey bucks.

17 As in 1.

18 Turn ears with palms out and bend your fingers as in the illustration.

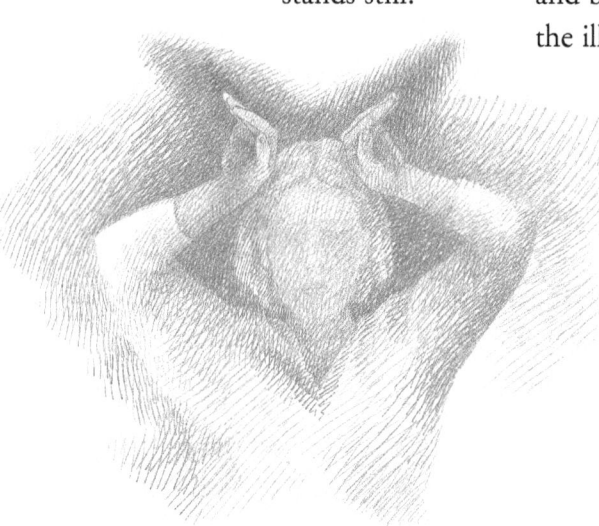

19 No-no, it's not his will,
   ← → ← →
   No – no – no!
   ← → ←
20 Calls: "Hee-ha-aw!"
               No, he does not
21 Want to move from
               this high spot.
   Headstrong,
               he stands quite still,
22 To move is not his will.
       ← →

23 My donkey wants to rest,
   Down in the grass is best.

19 With ears in the above position turn your head "no" to right and left. At the last "no," bend your head.

20 As in 1, but ears remain sideways. Call in a high note.

21 Form paws again and stand very stiff.

22 Relax along your whole body, paws remain in place. At "not his will," turn your lowered head slowly to right and left.

23 At "my donkey," lift your head tiredly, than let it sink again. Stand a while in this tired position. Then dissolve the paw gesture.

RESTING:

24 My donkey wants to rest.

25 He lies down in the
      grass to rest.

26 Down in the grass is best.

24 As in 22 and 23. This sentence may also be omitted.

25 Slowly kneel down on the floor.

26 From a kneeling position, completely lie down on your side on the floor, with your arms and legs lightly bent. After lying for a while, and after all the children are also resting, start singing the Rest-fifth song in a smooth, soft voice. Repeat by humming.

Rest-fifth: It is enough!

STREAMING   *TEXT AND MELODY: WILMA ELLERSIEK*

It is e-nough! It is e-nough for the lit - tle don-key dear.

He wants it to be qui - et here.

27 Comes a gentle wind,
    Phhhh! – Phhhh!

28 Softly strokes– soft and mild
    Phhhh! – Phhhh!
    The hide of the donkey child.
    Phhhh! – Phhhh!
    Softly strokes – soft and mild

27 Sit up slowly as quietly as possible. Speak the words very melodiously and allow your breath to escape without sound.

28 At "strokes," gently stroke the child closest to you across his/her side or back. Then rise carefully rise and go from child to child and

Phhhh! – Phhhh!
The hide of the donkey child.
Phhhh! – Phhhh! – Phhhhhhh!

stroke each "little donkey." Repeat the text until all children have been caressed. After the last child, lie quietly on the floor again. After a short pause, continue to speak:

29 The donkey,
      he has rested now!

29 Softly speak this sentence while still lying on the floor.

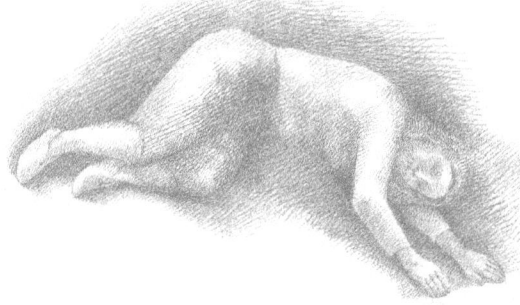

30 Stretches – stretches –

30 Stretch your arms and legs at right angles at the same time, forming your hands into fists. Then relax and bend arms and legs and repeat the stretching gesture. Pull arms and legs close to your body.

31 Rolls all around

31 Roll across your back to your other side.

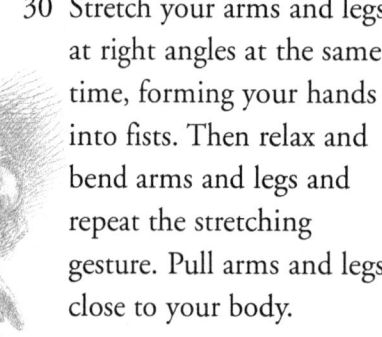

32 Gets up and stands
    On his legs again.

32 Get up on your hands and knees, then stand up with your hands as "paws," as in 1.

33 Rested now! Rested now!

34 The donkey stands and
             calls out free:
    "Hee-haw! Hee-ha-aw!"
    So happily!

33 Nod and call: "rested now!"
    in a high, happy voice.

34 As in 1.

Quawkalone and Brummelbone
Rhythmic-Musical Hand Gesture Game

He sits on a stone,
The froggy, Quawkalone!
Quaa – quaa – quax.

Bzzz-bzzz-bzzzzz!
Comes along fly Brummelbone.
Bzzz-bzzz-bzzzz!
Flies around frog Quawkalone.
Bzzzz-bzzzz-bzzzz-bzzzz!

Quawkalone goes: hop and snap!
Tasted tops! Tasted tops!
Happily, he licks his chops.
Quaa – quaa – quax!

Bzzz-bzzz-bzzzzz!
Comes another Brummelbone.
Bzzz-bzzz-bzzz!
Flies around frog Quawkalone.
Bzzzz-bzzzz-bzzzz-bzzzz!

Quawkalone goes: hop and snap!
Tasted tops! Tasted tops!
Happily, he licks his chops.
Quaa – quaa – quax!

Bzzz-bzzz-bzzzzz!
Comes another Brummelbone.
Bzzz-bzzz-bzzz!
Flies around frog Quawkalone.
Bzzzz-bzzzz-bzzzz-bzzzz!

Quawkalone goes: hop-
Ha-haaaa! Didn't snap!
Ha-haaaa! Didn't snap!

Bzzzz-bzzzz!
Off flies Brummelbone
To a different zone.
Bzzzz-bzzzz-bzzt!

And the froggy, Quawkalone,
Stays alone on his stone.
Quaa – quaa – quax!
And jumps: Splash!
Into his water home.

Or:

And rests alone.

TEXT:	HAND GESTURES:
1 He sits on a stone, The froggy, Quawkalone!	1 Sit on a stool or chair with closed knees as your playing board. During the game, your right hand is the frog and your left hand is the fly. At the sentence: "he sits on a stone" look happily at the children. At the word: "froggy," put down your right hand, with stretched, tightly closed fingers on your thigh close to your knee in such a way that only your wrist, the ball of your thumb, your thumb and your fingertips touch your leg. Your thumb is hidden in the hollow formed by the fact that all fingers lie across your thumb. Your fingertips face the children.

2   Quaa – quaa – quax.

2   Open the frog's mouth, with four stretched fingers, three times, each time as far as the mobility of your finger joints allow. Except for your fingers, your hand lies motionless on your thigh.

3   Bzzz-bzzz-bzzzzz!
    Comes along fly
            Brummelbone.

3   Make a loose fist with your left hand, stretching out your pointer. Your fingertip is the fly. From your left shoulder at "bzzz-bzzz-bzzz," the fly starts her flight in arcs of various sized in front of you. Sing the "bzzz" with sounding "zzz" at the same tone.

4   Bzzz-bzzz-bzzzzz!
    Flies around frog
            Quawkalone.
    Bzzzz-bzzzz-bzzzz-bzzzz!

4   As the frog sits motionless on his stone, the fly comes close and flies several times around him.

5   Quawkalone goes:
            hop and snap!

5   Suddenly, at the word: "hop," the frog comes to life. With one hop he snaps up the fly. Immediately thereafter, the frog sits again on his stone. Your left hand disappears unnoticed and hangs relaxed down at your left side.

6   Tasted tops! Tasted tops!
    ⟶ ⟵
    Happily, he licks his chops.
    ⟶ ⟵

6   The frog sits on his stone in such a way that only your curved wrist rests on your thigh. The children should be able to see well inside the frog's mouth. At the first "tasted tops," your thumb slowly rubs the inside of your hand from

	your pointer to your pinky, then back again during the second "tasted tops." Repeat this movement at the line: "happily, he licks his chops."
7 Quaa – quaa – quax!	7 As in 1 and 2.
8 Bzzz-bzzz-bzzzzz! Comes another Brummelbone. Bzzz-bzzz-bzzzzz! Flies around frog Quawkalone. Bzzzz-bzzzz-bzzzz-bzzzz! Quawkalone goes: hop and snap! Tasted tops! Tasted tops! Happily, he licks his chops. Quaa – quaa – quax!	8 Repeat everything from 3 – 7.
9 Bzzz-bzzz-bzzzzz! Comes another Brummelbone. Bzzz-bzzz-bzzzzz! Flies around frog Quawkalone. Bzzzz-bzzzz-bzzzz-bzzzz!	9 Repeat 3 and 4.
10 Quawkalone goes: hop – Ha-haaaa!	10 This time, the fly gets away from the frog. After the frog's leap, he returns to his original position and the fly continues to fly around in circles.
11 Didn't snap! Ha-haaaa! Didn't snap! Bzzzz-bzzzz! Off flies Brummelbone To a different zone. Bzzzz-bzzzz-bzzt!	11 The frog sits still unmoving on his stone, but the fly moves on in a lively fashion until he disappears behind your back as the "bzzz" become ever softer.
12 And the froggy, Quawkalone, Stays alone on his stone. Quaa – quaa – quax!	12 As in 2.

13 And jumps: Splash!
　　Into his water home.

Or:
And rests alone.

13 After the last "quax," make a fist with your right hand and rest it with your fingers on your thigh. At "jumps," bounce your right hand up while splaying your fingers wide. At the word "splash," slap your thighs with both hands, the frog has disappeared and your hands are hanging down at your side. Look happily at the children.

Before Dawn – Wake Up!
Rhythmic-Musical Hand Gesture Game

Before dawn, before dawn
Calls the rooster true: "Cock-a-doodle-doo!
Cock-a-doodle-doo! Wake up!" he cries,
"Wake up! The sun's about to rise!"

First wakes: "Tweet-tweet!" "Tweet-tweet!"
The birdie sweet: "Tweet-tweeeet!"

Then: "Ruff-ruff-ruff!" The doggy gruff.
"Ruff-ruff! – Ruff-ruff! – Ruff-ruff!"

He'll bray: "Hee-haw!" The donkey grey.
"Hee-haw! – Hee-haw! – Hee-haw!"

"Moo-moo!" are calling now
the ox and cow. "Moo-moo!"

And: "Meck-meck-may!" The billy-goat gay.
"Meck-meck! – Meck-meck! – Meck-may!"

In the warm and sunny light
Silently open the flowers bright.

At last, my children wake up, too
And laugh and laugh and laugh! Yoohoo!

TEXT:	HAND GESTURES:
1 Before dawn, before dawn	1 Turn joyfully to the children. Nod your head each time at "dawn."
2 Calls the rooster true: 　　　"Cock-a-doodle-doo! 　　　　　<　　　< 　　Cock-a-doodle-doo! 　　　<　　　< 　　　　Wake up!" he cries, 　　　　　<　　<	2 Your right hand is the rooster. Your stretched pointer lies on top of your stretched thumb forming a beak. Stretch and spread your other fingers as far as possible to form the rooster's comb. Sound the rooster call melodiously,

avoiding the interval of the third, opening the beak each time at "<."

3 "Wake up!
  The sun's about to rise!"

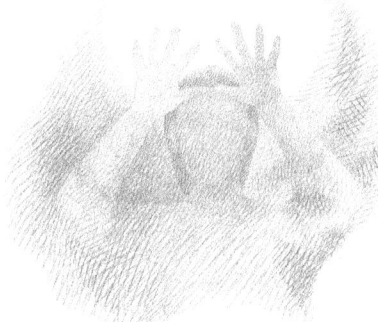

3 Hold your loose fists about chest height. Your thumbs touch and your curled fingers face forward to the children. Slowly move both arms upward together while straightening your fingers. Stop in front of your forehead and let the sun shine.

4 First wakes: "Tweet-tweet!"
       <   <
     "Tweet-tweet!"
       <   <
  The birdie sweet:
    <   <
     "Tweet-tweeeet!"
       <   <

4 Now your right hand is the birdie. Thumb and pointer form a "beak" as for the rooster, but this time your other fingers remain curled. Each time at "<," open the beak a little. At "<," open the beak wide and softly call "tweet." Call the second "tweet" a little longer.

5 Then: "Ruff-ruff-ruff!"
      ∠ ∠ ∠
  The doggy gruff.
     ∠ ∠
  "Ruff-ruff! – Ruff-ruff! –
  ∠ ∠   ∠ ∠
       Ruff-ruff!"
       ∠ ∠

5 Stretch all fingers of your right hand. Your thumb lies underneath your middle finger, fingertips point to the children. When the "doggy gruff" barks happily, open its mouth at "∠" just a little bit. At the

154

larger symbol "∠" it is opened wider and your voice is accordingly softer or louder. The bark is not naturalistic but musical using different intervals.

6   He'll bray: "Hee-haw!"
              The donkey grey.
     "Hee-haw! – Hee-haw! –
              Hee-haw!"

6   Hold your palms toward the children, fingers and thumbs tightly together and all fingers stretched into the fingertips. Now put your hands with the balls of your thumbs against the sides of your forehead as "donkey's ears." At "Hee," the "donkey" stretches upward from the waist, and at "Haw," resumes his original position. The donkey's call must be musical, not naturalistic, with the "Hee-haw" sounded as a fifth interval going down. At the word "donkey" lower your head a little. Then repeat "Hee-haw! - Hee-haw! - Hee-haw!" as above.

7   "Moo-moo!" are calling now
        ⊂   ⊂
     the ox and cow. "Moo-moo!"
        ⊂   ⊂   ⊂   ⊂

7   Form loose fists with both hands. Hold your left fist with the back of your hand toward the floor and lay your right fist, back up, on top of the left fist. This gesture is the mouth of the cow. At "moo," both wrists remain on top of each other, but both hands are moved back from the wrists, so that your curled fingers separate from each other. Open and close your

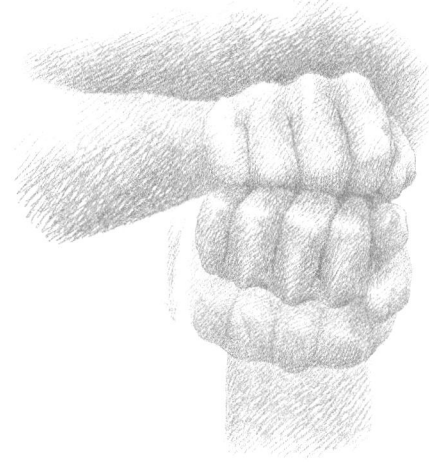

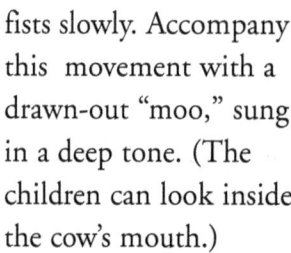

fists slowly. Accompany this movement with a drawn-out "moo," sung in a deep tone. (The children can look inside the cow's mouth.)

8   And: "Meck-meck-may!"
          x
    The billy-goat gay.
        x
    "Meck-meck! – Meck-meck! –
       x   x
               Meck-may!"
                    x

8   At the call "meck-meck-may," put each fist at the side of your forehead as "horns." Your thumbs lie outside your fingers and your pointers stick out straight. The "meck…" call should not be naturalistic, but musical, on the tone A. Speak the text very rhythmically and at each "x," nod slightly. For the last three "meck…" calls, nod first to the left, then to the right, and finally forward.

9   In the warm and sunny light

9   Hold both hands about forehead height with your stretched fingers spread, so that the thumb tips touch. For a while let the "sun" shine silently while leaning it forward a bit.

10   Silently open the flowers bright.

10   Each hand forms a bud by closely gathering all fingertips together as shown. Silently and very slowly separate your fingertips: the flower opens. Speak the text very drawn out. When the flowers are completely open, look at them and nod.

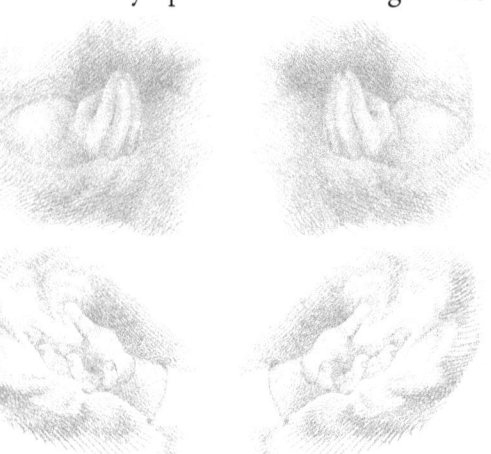

11 At last, my children
        wake up, too

12 And laugh and laugh
        and laugh! Yoohoo!

11 Rub your closed eyes. At the words: "wake up," take your hands from your eyes and look cheerfully at the children.

12 Stretch your upper body, lift your hands up to your head and turn your hands briskly in and out. After this, lower your hands and rest them on your thighs, keeping this resting position for a while.

Jingle Stick

Materials:

Dowel, 5/8" wide, 6" long, per stick.
Raffia or colored braid, 1 1/2" wide or 2 pieces, 3/4" wide.
4 brass jingles, 2 each with Ø 1/2" and Ø 3/4".
Round elastic.

Use jingles with metal balls as the tone producer. Larger jingles should not be used; their sound is too dominating.

Brass jingles with inner balls of metal are available at Nova Natural Toys and Crafts, see addresses p.161. They may also be for sale at the school store of your local Waldorf school.

Craft Directions:

Cut dowels to the right length, smoothing the cut ends with sand paper.

Drill holes through the dowel 1" and 2 1/4" from the dowel end.

Wrap the braid around the dowel, covering the drilled holes, and sew tightly together. The 1 1/2" wide braid will cover both holes, the 3/4" braid will cover one hole each.

Thread the round elastic into a needle and stitch it through the braid and a drilled hole. Stitch through the jingle loop and then back through drill hole and braid. Pull the elastic tight and knot the second jingle into it, very tightly. Repeat the same procedure for the second pair of jingles.

You may add a third pair of jingles to your own jingle stick. This will increase the sound, which is helpful in certain situations.

WILMA ELLERSIEK: A LIFE FOR RHYTHM

In a small village in Schleswig-Holstein, directly on the coastline of the Baltic Sea, on June 15, 1921, Wilma Ellersiek first saw the light of the world. With the rhythm of the waves, the murmur of the wind, and with dogs, cats, chickens, ducks and a horse as playmates, she lived a childhood bound up with nature. Her friends were, as she says, flowers, trees, sand and stars. But above all, rhythm, encountered at the seaside in many-layered forms, would stay with Wilma Ellersiek throughout her life. Looking back, she perceives her childhood as an almost heavenly life in the rhythm of nature. In her parents' home she was encouraged to pursue music, but also language and literature. Nature on one hand and culture on the other were an ideal, marvelous and edifying atmosphere for developing one's humanity.

In 1927 the Ellersiek family moved to Westphalia. Again little Wilma had the luck of living next-door to a farm; so the dear creatures remained her friends as before. New, however, was the impression of grain fields waving in the breeze, another rhythmic wave movement. Now came early meetings with other children, first in kindergarten and soon also in school. Their time together was filled with singing, dancing and recitation; indeed, looking back she sees her entire childhood and youth as suffused with music and rhythm, a sound basis for her later activity.

Wilma Ellersiek completed her schooldays with the *Abitur* examination and in 1941 she began to study in Leipzig, beginning in the major areas of school music, German philology and history of art. Serious sickness forced her to interrupt her study. This was followed by the confusion of wartime, near the end of which, in 1945, her

family was forced to flee from Eastern Europe. In Essen, Wilma Ellersiek resumed her study at the Volkwang School, albeit changing her major field. Her new field of study was rhythmic-musical education, continued in Stuttgart at the State Academy for Music and Performing Arts. There she became a student of Elfriede Feudel, herself a master student of the founder of "Eurhythmics," Émile Jacques-Dalcroze.[1] In addition to studying eurhythmics, Wilma Ellersiek also entered the study of speech education and completed both fields in 1957 with the state examination. Eurhythmics then became her life's content. She remained at the Stuttgart Music Academy as an assistant in the three departments: Eurhythmics, Theater and Spoken Word. After her time as assistant, she was offered a lecturing position, and later a professorship. In addition to her work at the Academy, she worked as stage director in opera and drama in Stuttgart, Vienna and London, among other places.

Again a serious sickness caused a decisive change in vocation, and again it was rhythm that fascinated her. Wilma Ellersiek now turned to research on the specific effects of rhythm and movement, language and music on the small child. Her work on this theme provoked attention, and in 1968 she received a research commission for it from the State of Baden-Württemberg. Out of this impulse the first "gesture-games" for the preschool child were born. Out of these little gesture-games, step-by-step, with enviable intuition, and also with enormous exactitude and care, she developed great, connected play-units in rhyme, interwoven with rhythm and music. In the beginning she called her courses "School for Parents," for her idea was to teach children together with mothers or fathers. In the late 1960's, the Stuttgart Music Academy established for Wilma Ellersiek, within the Eurhythmics Department, the specialty "Eurhythmics for the Preschool Age." During this time, a meeting took place with the "matriarch" of the Waldorf kindergartens, Klara Hattermann, with whom she maintained an intimate friendship. Klara Hattermann viewed the new games with interest, accompanied Wilma Ellersiek through many difficulties and encouraged again and again her continued activity. Along with several of Wilma Ellersiek's students from Stuttgart, Klara Hattermann has carried the games into the world through workshops. After twenty-five years of intensive teaching activity, Wilma Ellersiek retired, leaving the Academy in 1983. Lifted out of her teaching responsibilities, she became more creative than ever. Many of the games were developed at this time, among which are all the caresses and many lullabies. Additionally, during this time, a circle of interested friends came together in Hannover around Klara Hattermann to work intensively with the games of Wilma Ellersiek and see to their propagation in a form as true as possible to the intention of their author.

The games of Wilma Ellersiek come from her listening to Nature; in a way true to their origin she has succeeded in artistically molding speech, rhythm and the corresponding gestures to bring the wind, flowers, beasts, sun, moon and stars into the child's presence through little musical tales. In this way through the swinging, healing, natural rhythms of the games, she offers something to today's children from her own nature-filled childhood.

Ingrid Weidenfeld

---

[1] Dalcroze's Eurhythmics: not to be confused with the art of movement developed by Rudolf Steiner, called "Eurythmy."

Addresses

Waldorf Early Childhood Association of North America,
(WECAN)
285 Hungry Hollow Rd.
Spring Valley, NY 10977
Tel. (845) 352-1690
e-mail: info@waldorfearlychildhood.org

International Association of Steiner/Waldorf Early Childhood Education
PL 1800
S-15391 Järna, Sweden
Tel. 00-46-85-517-0250
Fax. 00-46-85-517-0685
Internet: www.waldorfkindergarten.de
E-Mail: geseke.lundgren@telia.com

Arbeitskreis der Ellersiek Spiele
Irmela Möller
An den Maschwiesen 2
30519 Hannover
E-Mail: s.weidenfeld@t-online.de

Lyn and Kundry Willwerth
2760 Webb Rd.
Cortland, NY 13045
Tel. (607) 756-2782
E-Mail: frauwillwerth@gmail.com

Choroi Instruments
available at:
Rudolf Steiner College Bookstore
9200 Fair Oaks Blvd.
Fair Oaks, CA 95628
Tel. (916) 961-8729

Nova Natural Toys and Crafts
140 Webster Rd.
Shelburne, VT 05482
Tel. (802) 985-8300
E-Mail: ted@novanatural.com

Learning CDs for *Giving Love - Bringing Joy* and
Gesture Games for Spring and Summer, Autumn and Winter
available at:
Hillside Kindergarten
2760 Webb Rd.
Cortland, NY 13045
Tel. (607) 756-2782
E-Mail: frauwillwerth@gmail.com

Giving Love – Bringing Joy
Hand Gesture Games and Lullabies in the Mood of the Fifth

By Wilma Ellersiek
Edited and translated by Kundry and Lyn Willwerth
Illustrations by Friedericke Lögters
110 pages with Spiral binding.
Publisher: WECAN

The first volume of Wilma Ellersiek's *Hand Gestures, Songs and Movement Games* offers lighthearted, gentle touch games for expectant mothers, parents and caregivers to play with their infants, toddlers and young children, strengthening love and confidence in the world.

These touch games, called "caresses" by Wilma Ellersiek, consist of rhymed verses or lullabies and gentle, caressing touches as were practiced in similar folk games which have fallen into disuse in today's media society.

Her lullabies are based on the experience of the fifth interval with central tone A and are often accompanied by corresponding hand gestures.

Gesture Games for Spring and Summer
Hand Gesture Games, Songs and Movement Games for Children in Kindergarten and the Lower Grades

By Wilma Ellersiek
Edited and translated by Kundry and Lyn Willwerth
Illustrations by Friedericke Lögters
136 pages with Spiral binding.
Publisher: WECAN

Poets and musicians alike have been inspired to celebrate the renewal of spring and its fulfillment in summer.

We all know that young children show a spontaneous interest in every little ant or pebble that needs to be touched and explored. In sharing the experiences of the innumerable small wonders of nature with our children we can awaken in them feelings of love, concern and responsibility for the life of our planet.

These songs, hand gestures and movement games for the seasons of spring and summer by Wilma Ellersiek lead our children to joyful participation and understanding of nature around them.

Gesture Games for Autumn and Winter
Hand Gesture Games, Songs and Movement Games for Children in Kindergarten and the Lower Grades

By Wilma Ellersiek
Edited and translated by Kundry and Lyn Willwerth
Illustrations by Friedericke Lögters
146 pages with Spiral binding.
Publisher: WECAN

When the colored leaves are blown about by gale and rain, fog envelops us in the morning and soon the first snow falls, then our children can be part of these events by playing the games offered in this book by Wilma Ellersiek. These rhythmic-musical verses, songs and circle games are artistically created representations of the events in nature.

As children become familiar with the wonder of each season, they and their parents and caregivers, in playing these games, will experience the rustling wind, blizzard and frost, the stillness of the snow-covered world, with heightened sensitivity.

In the warmth of our home and pre-school we can play at skating on the frozen pond, building a snowman, even celebrating Halloween, thanks to the hand gesture and movement games by Wilma Ellersiek, presented in this volume.

www.ingramcontent.com/pod-product-compliance
Lightning Source LLC
Chambersburg PA
CBHW081722100526
44591CB00016B/2468